One Long, *Wild* Conversation

To a respected colleague and
an excellent graduate student
Best wishes to ~~Hare~~ and Ruth from Bob

Fraser ~~Drew~~
1 May 2009

For David and Ruth ~~Lampe~~ —
In respect and
admiration for your gifts
to BSC Special Collections.

Hank Harper
5-1-09

One Long, *Wild* Conversation

Selected Letters Between
a Buffalo State Professor and
His Student, a Writer

Edited by
Fraser Drew & Hank Nuwer

Buffalo State College   Buffalo, NY

A joint publication of E. H. Butler Library and
the Monroe Fordham Regional History Center

For ease of reading, where material has been cut or edited, the letters contain no ellipsis or brackets for the sake of readability. All letters contain the dates on which they were written, but information on where they were written is included only where useful to the text to avoid redundancy. Some of Drew's attachments to Nuwer containing memoirs were added to certain letters to flesh out allusions to events in his life. Drew's preference in dating letters is day, month, year; Nuwer's preference is month, day, year.

Front cover photograph by Jenine Howard.

Layout and design by Dennis Reed, Jr.

Buffalo State College   Buffalo, NY
A joint publication of E. H. Butler Library and the Monroe Fordham Regional History Center

Fraser Drew:

For Jim Brophy, and in memory of my father and mother, and my teachers.

Hank Nuwer:

For Adam Robert Drew Nuwer, the namesake of Fraser Drew, Christian Cerniglia, President Muriel A. Howard of Buffalo State College, and my friend Maryruth Glogowski of BSC's Butler Library.

"The class was just one long, wild conversation. Frost made some of us uncomfortable, forcing us to look at subjects honestly and address them in our own voice, but we admired him."

—Former student of Robert Frost (*The Art of Teaching* by Jay Parini)

CONTENTS

Foreword by Fraser Drew

Hank Nuwer and I go back to 1964 after I left the chairmanship of the English Department after two terms, and he was planning to play freshman baseball and take a degree in social studies. One day he appeared at my office in Ketchum Hall to request my signature as a Sigma Tau Rho faculty brother on a wooden plaque, an archaic ritual kept from Rho's predecessor, Sigma Tau Gamma.

I remembered him when he came to my Contemporary Literature class the following semester. Hank quickly became one of the most productive students in the class, joining discussions and writing excellent examination papers. As one of two or three students to receive an A grade, he received a book of poetry inscribed for him by its writer, in this case the New York and New Jersey poet Louise Townsend Nicholl.

As Hank changed his major at Buffalo State to English and went on for a master's degree at New Mexico Highlands University and additional graduate work at the University of Nevada, then taught in South Carolina, Virginia, and Indiana, we stayed in touch. He sent me copies of some of the nearly two thousand newspaper, magazine and online articles he wrote, and in time, his fiction manuscripts and his books on contemporary writers, sports, and hazing reforms. Sometimes these were dedicated to me, or I shared dedications with members of his family, or other friends. I was delighted by his expanding powers as a writer and by the praise he received as a journalist and a teacher of journalism and nonfiction writing.

Among the happiest events in his life were the births of Hank's sons, Christian and Adam, and I was especially pleased by the middle names that he gave to Adam: Robert and Drew. As his teacher I was delighted, too, when Buffalo State College gave him its Distinguished Alumnus Award in 1999 and in 2006 an honorary Doctor of Letters degree from the SUNY system.

More than any other English major in my decades of teaching, Hank has experienced success and acclaim, especially for his authoritative speaking and writing on hazing in modern life. He has also demonstrated more frequently and convincingly than any other, his gratitude for my assistance, encouragement and friendship. He is the ideal example of the pupil who moves beyond the achievements of a mentor but carries with him the smiling companionship of the man who was his teacher.

Back in May 1979 I published an essay for *College English* that contained my thoughts on teaching inspired by a single memorable visit to talk with poet Robert Frost about poetry, teaching, and other matters that I delighted to bring into my classroom for students such as Nuwer to embrace. Always I was reminded of the famous Frost quote about successful teaching, namely, "All the fun is in how you say the thing." He also told me this: "Don't teach them a lesson, show them a lesson."

Occasionally it happens that the dialog begun in a classroom between teacher and student transcends the college experience and continues in a lifetime of correspondence. The volume in your hands contains just such a lifetime of responses between Hank Nuwer and myself. A few years of corresponding were lost or thrown away, unfortunately, but the majority of Drew-Nuwer letters between 1970 and 2008 remain intact.

I hope you enjoy them, perhaps thinking of yourself as one of those silent but brilliant souls in a classroom who never speaks but soaks up all.

Preface by Hank Nuwer

The idea for putting together a volume of letters between State University of New York Distinguished Professor of English Fraser Drew and me, one of the more than 12,000 Buffalo State students he influenced in the classroom, flamed into something more than a mere notion when that professor, Fraser Drew, returned two boxes of my letters to him. He had reduced his possessions before making what he called his "final address change" into a retirement community.

I took the correspondence I had sent him from 1970 to 2008 and mixed it in chronological order with letters from Drew over the same time period. I long ago had organized these by year. The folders filled two drawers of a file cabinet.

That task accomplished, Professor Drew and I began to edit nearly one million words. We discarded letters that were so personal so as to interest only the writers. We included those letters, or portions thereof, that seemed to illustrate the literary passion of two friends united in the belief that literature, classroom instruction, and libraries mattered. We retained some letters containing enough autobiographical material to reveal our personalities. Thus, some of these letters we exchanged over time refer to loss and heartache, family matters, and changes over the years at Buffalo State College.

Moreover, we wanted this book to reflect the conviction that letter writing is an important ritual in human life that must not be allowed to disappear in this era of disposable email and cell phone text messaging. I hardly was the only author that Drew exchanged letters with in his lifetime. The correspondence between Drew and Langston Hughes, Ernest Hemingway, John Masefield, Robert Frost, Robinson Jeffers and Thornton Wilder has been of value not only to literary biographers, but is to all readers of those biographies, and that is why Drew generously gave (or will give) these materials to Library Special Collections at the University of Vermont and Buffalo State College. Likewise, influenced by my mentor's unselfishness, the letters and notes sent to me over four decades from such well-known writers as Kurt Vonnegut, James Dickey, Jesse Stuart and Maurice Sendak now repose in Butler Library as my gift to the college for future scholars and student term paper writers.

We editors began this volume with a chronology 1913-1970, covering the years from Drew's birth to the first letter between the English professor and me—a fledgling writer burning to dismantle the barricade blocking the world of publishing. I hoped that the knowledge that I floundered for more than a decade as a writer might inspire persistence worth the cultivating in future writers who may read this book.

For every author whose overnight success has turned him or her into household names, thousands of so-called "midlist" authors such as Louise Townsend Nicholl have had to measure success, not in volumes sold, but rather in the belief that what we do for a living makes a difference to someone, somewhere.

Some of that belief, I hope, comes through in the references in these letters to Drew that reflect my insistence on publishing articles and books on hazing prevention. Those passages in these letters represent my faith that society one day will halt deaths and indignities associated with the medieval practice of hazing. As scholar Michael Kimmel noted in his 2008 book *Guyland*, since the 1970s I've been on "a virtual one-man crusade to eliminate hazing."

These letters connecting the Drew-Nuwer friendship have

been postmarked from many different U.S. states and countries such as Belgium, Germany, England, the Dominican Republic, Canada, Mexico, Spain, Switzerland, Luxembourg and Italy. Those letters from him have found me—sometimes with two and three forwards on the envelope—while I put together a writing portfolio of 24 books and some 2,000 articles and reviews.

Often while compiling these letters I kept thinking back to my inauspicious first day in Drew's classroom. He began his lecture while I finished telling a joke to a female student, and he switched my seat to a chair in front of him.

Not that he was a disciplinarian by any means, mainly because he never had to be. He held the attention of even a class loaded with athletes. He had this engaging way of making both the works of literature and their creators come to life as he talked, and he did it nearly every class, not just when he taught something in his expertise. He had a developed sense of humor, once breaking into gusty laughter when my fraternity brother John Vasi brought an Irish wolfhound to a final exam in Irish literature. "I spent the whole time petting the dog," Drew later said with a chuckle, retelling the story many years later.

Over time the love of literature I developed at Buffalo State College gave me the background I needed when I began interviewing writers for various periodicals. These authors and poets included well-known literary figures such as Norman Mailer, Nikki Giovanni, Harry Crews, George Plimpton, Howard Nemerov, Michael Lee West and William Least Heat Moon, but also writers of popular prose such as Diana Gabaldon, Rex Stout, Mickey Spillane, Rosemary Rogers and John Jakes.

Drew taught modern English, Irish and American literature. He has pooh-poohed his role in my development as a writer, but nonetheless he was very important. He showed me how authentic writers and poets never were satisfied with their first or even fifth drafts, scratching away chaff to get to the wheat. I learned from him that skilled rewriting and inspired collaboration between writer and editor made the difference in whether a manuscript stayed

Preface by Hank Nuwer

unpublished in a desk drawer or found publication and possibly acclaim.

Professor Drew and I hope you enjoy these letters by two ordinary men who sought two lifetimes of fulfillment in books and exploration. If you pick up a pen and write those in your life who matter to you instead of clicking a text message that soon will be lost in cyberspace, we will judge this book of letters well worth the creating.

Introductory Chronology

This chronology preceding the first letters between Drew and Nuwer begins with the birth of Fraser (Bob) Drew in 1913. Additional chronological notes are found among the letters to provide context. The selected passages are taken from more than 1,500 Drew-Nuwer letters and biographical attachments sent to one another between 1970 and 2008.

1913 Fraser Bragg ("Bob") Drew was born June 23, 1913, in Randolph, Vermont.

1929 Fraser Drew was class valedictorian at Randolph High School in 1929. At sixteen, he enrolled at the University of Vermont. His dog Bing, a well-mannered collie-Newfoundland mix, stayed at Drew's Lambda Iota fraternity house and accompanied him to classes.

1932 Drew was elected to Phi Beta Kappa in his junior year. He was editor in chief of the *Vermont Cynic* newspaper; president of Lambda Iota fraternity, a member of the rifle team, and president of Boulder, the senior leadership society.

That same year, poet Hart Crane killed himself by diving into the Gulf of Mexico from a cruise ship. Drew later collected Crane books, letters, and memorabilia, including Crane's sombrero that the poet had purchased in Mexico before his death.

1933 Drew received his A.B. *magna cum laude*, University of Vermont.

1935 Duke University conferred the A.M. degree on Drew with a major in Latin, a minor in Greek. His thesis was "Horace and the Schools of Greek Philosophy."

1936 Drew heard about a job vacancy at Green Mountain College through serendipity. Drew's mother had stopped at the home of the Congregational minister in Randolph where Jesse Parker Bogue, the president of Green Mountain College, chanced to visit. Drew was hired by Bogue and was voted "Favorite Instructor" by GMC students, the vote influenced by his passion for dancing the "Tiger Rag" at campus dances.

1937 Drew's interest in John Masefield began at Green Mountain College. He came upon a signed copy of *King Cole* in a bookstore and began collecting first-edition copies of *Dauber*, *Reynard the Fox*, and the other Masefield narratives.

1938 Drew's beloved dog Bing died. Bing had become a Randolph town fixture, and his obituary ran in the White River *Herald*. He was buried beneath a white birch on the property of Drew's parents.

1939 The White River *Herald* in 1939 carried this headline: "Randolph Youths Escape Death as Car Strikes Horse." According to the *Herald*, "The heavy work horse was catapulted completely over Hodges' light roadster. The imprint of hoofs is visible on the back of the seat where [Fraser] Drew sat."

Drew completed thirty hours of graduate school credit in English at Syracuse University, attending from 1939 through 1941. A favorite professor was Gladys Rose Bikle, who taught the modern novel, charming him with the ever-present quiet hat with veil she wore to class.

1941-1945 World War Two interrupted Drew's graduate school plans. He worked during the war as a foreman in a naval aircraft plant in Hartford, Connecticut, getting to his appointed rounds in the huge building on a tricycle. He audited a Shakespeare class taught by scholar Odell Shepard at Trinity College.

1945 BSC hired Drew as an instructor in English.

1946 Hank Nuwer was born on August 19 in Buffalo.

1948 On June 1 John Masefield replied to a letter from Drew, leading to continued correspondence and Drew's Masefield collection.

1949 While researching the life and work of John Masefield, Drew discovered a 1919 essay on the poet written by Louise Townsend Nicholl, a poet and an editor for E.P. Dutton of novelists Gore Vidal and Jesse Stuart. Drew and Nicholl became friends.

1950 One morning the resident collie dog at the Homer Noble Farm in Ripton, Vermont led Drew up the hill to Robert Frost's cabin. The poet gave Drew an audience, a favor to a fellow Vermonter. After a conversation in which Frost admonished Drew to "show" students a lesson, not tell them what they needed to know, the poet signed the teacher's copy of *Mountain Interval* with a printer error on page 88. Frost crossed out the offending line, wrote in the correct words, signed the correction and dated it. Then Frost wrote the first eight lines of "The Road Not Taken" in the book and gave Drew a signed photograph.

Also in 1950, a June 22 letter from Una Jeffers, wife of poet Robinson Jeffers, led Drew to begin another literary collection and to maintain friendship with the poet and Jeffers family. On June 25, a first letter from Ernest Hemingway arrived, the first of many written to Drew.

1952 Drew was promoted to full professor at Buffalo State. He completed his dissertation defense for the Ph.D. in English at the University of Buffalo.

1953 Fraser Drew's mother died on February 18.

1955 Drew visited Ernest Hemingway in Cuba at the Finca Vigia. This visit was noted by Hemingway biographer Carlos Baker. The writer took Drew to his office and pointed out his typewriter atop a bookshelf where he typed while standing. Hemingway gave Drew a sack of signed books for himself, his father, and three students. Drew had come up with the idea of starting an annual contemporary literature award, giving his best students copies of signed volumes by writers. Hemingway talked about his convalescence from a plane crash and wished that he could have taken Drew on a fishing cruise. "Writers are always a disappointment when you meet them," Hemingway said. "All the good in them goes into their books, and they are dull themselves."

1957 Drew assumed the chair of English at Buffalo State. He served through 1963.

1959 In the State Historical Society in Montpelier, Vermont, Drew saw Lord Byron's sword on display. He tracked its origin and journey to the museum in an issue of *Vermont History* that year.

1960 Nuwer attended the Diocesan Preparatory Seminary to see if he had a vocation.

1962 Nuwer was expelled from the seminary in March. In addition to failing grades, he had disciplinary run-ins with his algebra teacher, the Reverend Paul Belzer, later the confessor to future Oklahoma City bomber Timothy McVeigh and the family of McVeigh. Nuwer enrolled at Cheektowaga Central High School.

1963 The Buffalo *Evening News* paid Nuwer for a television review and a short essay.

1964 Drew toured Ireland, Scotland and England. He made six more visits to Ireland between 1967 and 1979. One of his memorable excursions was to the 16th century Norman castle and tower of William Butler Yeats at Thoor Ballylee, an important symbol in Yeats' poetry.

That summer, in England, Drew talked by phone with the poet John Masefield at his Berkshire home in the Thames Valley. Drew also traveled to the haunts of Geoffrey Chaucer and Thomas Malory, Robert Burns, Byron, Thomas Hardy, and A. E. Housman.

Nuwer turned 18 on August 19 and entered BSC to study social studies, commuting to campus with his Cheektowaga high school friend Joe Nikiel.

1965 In June of 1965 Drew and Jim Brophy purchased a home in Tonawanda and acquired a German shepherd named Wolf.

In a freshman writing class, Nuwer persuaded English instructor Annette T. Rottenberg to let him write a long parody of the James Bond novels by Ian Fleming in place of one regular "Effective Communication" assignment. It was the first creative writing he attempted.

1967 Drew and Jim Brophy obtained an audience with Irish President Éamon de Valera in Dublin at the president's office at Aras an Uachtarain in Phoenix Park.

Nuwer worked nights in a coke mill while taking a Drew summer literature class during the day. Drew agreed to read a file of unpublished poems and light verse that Nuwer had written in the last year, and the professor gave him guarded encouragement.

1968 The University of Vermont awarded Drew a Distinguished Alumnus Award. He presented his Masefield collection to Bailey/Howe Library at the University of Vermont.

Nuwer graduated from Buffalo State College. Drew awarded him one of the annual Contemporary Literature book awards. In his first summer out of school, he worked three months in New York City as a security guard, once watching over a private collection of Salvatore Dali paintings and, for one memorable afternoon, shadowing the Duke and Duchess of Windsor on a shopping expedition. Nuwer married fellow BSC student Alice Cerniglia of Brooklyn, New York.

1969 Nuwer published his writings and reviews in newspapers, small-press poetry magazines, and low-circulation national periodicals. He interviewed mystery novelist Rex Stout at the writer's hilltop home in Brewster, New York. He wrote about the Woodstock Music Festival, the 1969 Washington Peace March, and the New York tickertape parade for moon-landing astronauts.

1970 Nuwer thought a career in college teaching combined with writing sounded like the ideal career. He consulted his former BSC professor Fraser (Bob) Drew to ask advice and to share his plans. Nuwer entered New Mexico Highlands University as a teaching fellow to pursue an M.A. in English.

PART I

Professor to Graduate Student

(1970-1975)

1. Hank Nuwer to Fraser Drew
Carmel, New York
February 1, 1970

Dear Dr. Drew:

I realize that it has been three years since I last had a class with you, but I thought that I would take a moment to tell you that the classes I had under you have greatly influenced my life.

In the first place, the encouragement you gave me with my attempts at poetry has enabled me to publish a few poems, and to take up writing as a career. I am now a reporter for the *Reporter Dispatch* covering Westchester and Putnam Counties, a columnist for the weekly *Putnam County Courier*, and a freelance staff humor writer for Caldor Publications. The money is low, but I am having a good time meeting people, traveling and writing. I was married in December 1968. I kept up your policy of mailing out first editions of books, and my library has swollen considerably after starting a book review column.

Next fall I hope to go west to graduate school. I have nine hours of graduate credit from Western Connecticut College and the University of Bridgeport to transfer that I have squeezed into my schedule last spring and summer. My eventual aim is to teach college and write. The last I heard though, Joyce Carol Oates has not lost any sleep over fear that my literary talents will overtake her.

At any rate, I just felt like sending my regards. Attached you will find a book review I did of the new Robert Frost volume. The review describes one of the many class lectures of yours I enjoyed while at Buffalo State.

Cordially,

Henry Nuwer

2. Drew to Nuwer
Buffalo State College
22 February 1970

Dear Henry,

Your letter of three weeks ago deserved a much quicker response. I can't remember when a letter has given me more pleasure. It was good to know that former student is engaged in interesting work and is happily married, that he remembers his classes with me, and that he is thoughtful enough to write and tell me so and to send concrete evidence of the fact! What more could a teacher ask?

If you do go on to a combination of college teaching and writing, both these early jobs will be of great value to you. Good luck, and remember that you may use my name at any time in making application for graduate school or other work.

Congratulations on your marriage! I wish you every happiness. I am still (and apparently forever) a bachelor, but my German shepherd dog is the joy of my life.

I liked your Frost review very much, and of course I was delighted to appear in it. It is a good review and I can tell that you enjoy your writing. I have put the review into my own "Collected Frost."

Buffalo State is larger and livelier than ever. There are times when I would gladly turn back the calendar a bit, and there are probably times ahead when I'll feel even more strongly about the "good old days." But I'm still enjoying my job. I now spend half time helping the new chairman, Henry Sustakoski, as I used to help Stephen Sherwin, my successor at the chairman's job. I teach one section of good old Contemporary lit and one graduate course, either Irish lit, or [Robinson] Jeffers-and-[E.A.] Robinson.

Eire-Ireland: A Journal of Irish Studies has published four serious articles in the past two years, and my other writing has been travel essays for *Ireland of the Welcomes*, *In Britain*, and *Buffalo Evening News Magazine*. Right now, however, I'm working on a Hemingway piece of some length. I've given my Masefield collection (some 500 first editions, 200 letters, etc.) to the University of Vermont in memory of my favorite professor and another friend there. I intend to take my fourth trip to Ireland this coming May-June. I want to do a little research, see some friends, revisit loved spots and see some new ones, especially in the far southwest (County Kerry) and in Galway, Mayo and of course Dublin's fair city.

Page end. No more now. But my appreciative thanks and best wishes,

Fraternally,

Bob Drew

3. Nuwer to Drew
Carmel, New York
February 23, 1970

Thank you very much for the Robert Frost picture. Alice will have it framed on my office wall, which now has posters/clippings of John Masefield, Archibald MacLeish, another Frost photo, a large Hemingway poster, Mark Twain, William Shakespeare. From the choice of decorations, you can readily tell how much influence you have had in generating enthusiasm for your favorite authors.

The Mark Twain photo reflects my interest stirred by Dr. Martin Fried's classes. The other two English teachers who left an impression on me were Dr. Cleveland Jauch and Dr. Wilson Gragg. From my student teaching I guess I will always remember Dr. Mehl who frightened me as much as helped me. He always appeared so stern, but he was very willing to discuss any aspect of teaching.

I learned that [W.H.] Auden had used a family named Nower as a key part of one of his major plays. I believe the title was *Paid*. Did you know that the *New York Times* published an article on Masefield in the Friday, January 9, 1970 issue?

I'll be in Buffalo to see the draft board soon. I am 1-A now with Lottery Number 311.

On another topic, did you read the *Times* newspaper clipping in December that said Ireland hoped to create a tax-free haven for poets, writers, and painters?

I hope to attend New Mexico Highlands University in the fall. It would be great if I could get an assistantship, but the tuition is not unreasonable if I cannot. So far I have an "A" average for nine graduate hours, and all are transferable. I'm keeping my fingers crossed.

I have [attached] a stamped, addressed envelope to New Mexico Highlands University. If you could find time to write a recommendation for me I would greatly appreciate your trouble. Again, I cannot thank you enough for the Frost gift.

Very truly yours,

Henry Nuwer

1971 On June 13 Drew attended a memorial service in the Church of the Most Holy Trinity on the grounds of Dublin Castle for Irish revolutionary Michael Collins, shot in the head and killed on August 22, 1922. Drew was moved at the sight of aged men who had fought alongside "The Big Fella," carrying the tattered banners they had raised in their youth.

Nuwer graduated from Highlands in August with an M.A. in English and then taught in an experimental federal grant-supported writing program with students of Mexican-American heritage at Highlands University in conjunction with West Las Vegas High School. At NMHU, Nuwer's best writing student was Victoria Sanchez, later to become a college professor herself, and her uncle was Joe Robert Sanchez, WLVH principal, and an important teaching mentor for Hank.

Nuwer formed a friendship with the octogenarian cowboy poet, novelist, and *Overland Monthly* and *Saturday Evening Post* contributor S. Omar Barker (1885-1985). Barker visited Nuwer's high school classes and led the students in light verse "cowboy poetry" writing. Nuwer also met the fiery Reies López Tijerina, radical leader of the Chicano movement, an advocate of restoring land grants to the original owners of Mexican descent.

1972 Nuwer accepted University of Nevada assistantship award money, excited by what he wrongly thought was the faculty presence of Walter Van Tilburg Clark, author of *The Ox-bow Incident,* and an acquaintance of Drew's when both attended the University of Vermont. Unknown to Nuwer, Clark had passed away in November 1971, taking away Nuwer's primary purpose in going to graduate school in Reno.

Henry Christian Nuwer was born to Hank and Alice Cerniglia Nuwer on September 15, 1972.

4. Nuwer to Drew
Las Vegas, New Mexico
April 14, 1972

Dear Dr. Drew:

Once again I must write you to thank you for giving me sound advice. Despite your efforts, the University of Buffalo turned me down [for admission to graduate school], and I would have been without a position for September if I hadn't written to additional schools as you suggested. About two hours ago, one of my second choice schools, the University of Nevada, offered me a teaching fellowship beginning August 24th. A Prof. Robert Harvey of the English Department phoned and asked if I was available yet. Needless to say, I didn't hold out for a bonus or a new car. The stipend is for $2,700 and remission of all tuition and fees.

It really seems funny how luck runs in streaks. Today I received a letter in the mail from the editor of the *South Dakota Review* giving me the go ahead to do an interview with Western writer Jack Warner Schaefer [the author of *Shane*]. At this stage I am happy for the opportunity to get anything published at any time so that my dossier will look a little better when I'm finally ready to hunt for a college teaching position.

I will take whatever summer job pays the most money because my wife Alice is expecting a baby come September.

We will make the trip to Reno in our 1955 Dodge, which appears to be in better shape than many of the new cars Ralph Nader has been investigating.

About the only other thing new is that my new beard is getting quite long. I guess it's a good thing too. The hair on top is getting quite sparse. "Uneasy lies the head that is losing its crown," as the new saying goes.*

Oh, I forgot. I'm also trying to write a juvenile book. Like Jack London I am trying to put down 1,000 words per day. Unlike Jack London, nine-tenths of my words get blotted out.

Well, thank you again for writing those references and for sending that cheery letter last month. My wife and I hope that you are well and happy. If you find time, send a postcard from Ireland. Oh yes, would you be kind to send along a small bibliography of your latest publications?

I did manage to find a letter of yours from Robinson Jeffers published in *The Selected Letters of Robinson Jeffers*. However, I have not been lucky enough to come across the Hemingway pieces or Frost articles you wrote. My wife and I would like very much to read them and if you can send the title and month of the issues they were in, I will write each magazine for reprints or old issues.

Well, I guess I have just about typed your ear off with my chattering. So this will be all for now.

Cordially, Hank

*Ed. The line came from an unpublished light verse poem Nuwer had written.

5. Nuwer to Drew
Las Vegas, New Mexico
July 26, 1972

Dear Dr. Drew:

We leave for Nevada in a few days. School starts August 22.

My wife has had a difficult summer. She graduates and gives birth to our firstborn during September. The trip to Reno will not be easy on her. I hope that our '55 Dodge can withstand the heat. Everything else is fine, however.

Did you go to Ireland this summer? Has your new book been published yet? Hope this finds you and your father in good health.

I had a poem in this month's issue of *New Mexico Magazine* and will have an article in the spring or summer issue of the *South Dakota Review*. We have a large two-bedroom duplex on the California-Nevada border. If you ever have the urge to visit Lake Tahoe, Yosemite, or Virginia City, you are very welcome to stay here. I assure you that my wife is a good cook.

Well, I guess I will close for now. I hope that your fall semester is a successful one.

Best regards,

Hank Nuwer

6. Nuwer to Drew
University of Nevada
November 7, 1972

Dear Professor Drew:

Thought that I would drop a short note to you to see how you are and to let you know that your influence is still being felt by me. I am working on a paper for a seminar on Walter Van Tilburg Clark and am doing a comparison on Robinson Jeffers' poetry and Clark's writings while he was a student at Nevada and Vermont. The paper will also deal with Jeffers' influences upon Clark's fiction.

I have collected all of Clark's published poetry, and a half dozen (including one of 130 pages) unpublished poems into one manuscript.

It has been a lot of fun to do, and has given me the opportunity to read most of Jeffers' published poems and a good deal of criticism on him, including an interesting article on the gentle side of R.J. by a certain professor at the SUCNY at Buffalo which I enjoyed very much and quoted in my term paper.

I am going to do a dissertation on Clark, hopefully a full length biography.*

Clark was a teacher first and then a writer, but he has two fine novels (and one bad novel, *The City of Trembling Leaves*) and a vast amount of published through uncollected short stories to plow through.

Our son, H. Christian, is fine. My wife is in good health. Our hours are funny now. I usually sleep evenings, study nights, and teach/go to classes during the day.

We did have a bad moment on Sunday. An air bubble apparently got into the brake fluid of my 1955 Dodge, and I barreled into an intersection at twenty miles an hour, missing any pedestrians but slamming into two autos. My car and a Mustang were demolished and a station wagon was severely damaged. All of us were bruised but luckily, no one was hospitalized. My insurance should pay for the damage to the other drivers' cars.

Other than that all is well in Reno. My library is continuing to grow although a good deal of it is stored [with Alice's parents] in Newburgh, New York and I definitely miss having these books. Hope that your classes are fun for you this semester, and that your publications are finding a home in various journals.

Best Regards,

Hank Nuwer

Ed. The biography was turned down by Nuwer's doctoral committee, as not acceptable as a form of original scholarship. Nuwer has discovered that his choice of UNR for doctoral study was a bad fit.

7. Nuwer to Drew
University of Nevada
November 22, 1972

Dear Professor Bob:

I was very excited over receiving the three Xerox copies of Clark's letters,* and I have already started saving my pennies to purchase a copy of *John Masefield's England.*

I hope one day to have a library to rival yours. It now numbers over 2,000 hardcover books, but with only a few signed editions. At the present time I am working on my dissertation and getting to meet writers by interviewing Clark experts for the *Sagebrush* student newspaper here at UNR.

Occasionally UNR has guest speakers here and I interview them too. UNR is a good school for me in one respect: I've been able to do all the interviews I want. This year I have (or will) interview author

Wallace Stegner, Chicago 7 attorney William Kunstler, critic Max Westbrook, poet Gary Snyder, and poet Ezekiel Mphahlele. Obviously it will take me decades to come close to your fine collection and perhaps I never will do so—but you have given me a goal to shoot for and the encouragement you have given me since 1966 has been the major reason I have gone on for the Ph.D.

I only wish that I could have the good fortune to have had more professors who cared about their students the way you have for your people. I have one excellent teacher, Prof. Charlton Laird, and one good teacher, Dr. Robert Hume, but they lack your enthusiasm for life and literature. It looks like two other fellows (Bill Baines and Kelsie T. Harder) and I will edit the literary magazine here.

One exciting thing has happened lately. I have received permission from UNR Special Collections to examine Walter Van Tilburg Clark letters and poems that have never been published on condition that I not publish them without permission.** I have included one poem here that I thought would interest you. I just thought that you might enjoy reading it privately since you knew both Jeffers and Clark.

I guess that is all for now. You are probably getting reader's cramp by now. Thank you once again for favoring me with the letters. Hope this letter finds you well and happy. My wife Alice sends her regards: Chris sends the flicker of a smile. My dog Fagin greets you with a woof!

Best regards,

Hank Nuwer

*Ed. Drew sent Nuwer copies of three letters Walter Van Tilburg Clark had sent him.

**Ed. The Clark poem "For Robinson Jeffers was attached, and Nuwer later obtained permission from Clark's son Robert to print it in Brushfire, the UNR literary magazine.

8. Nuwer to Drew
University of Nevada
December 13, 1972

Dear Professor Bob:

Just thought I would drop a short note to wish you Merry Christmas.

Attached is an interview I conducted hot off the press with critic Robert Heilman of the University of Washington. *Janus Magazine*, a magazine that publishes one-act plays, accepted a play of mine titled "Beyond Survival," a social satire.

I wonder if I might ask advice, The graduate committee I was given has no published professors except for a few isolated publications here and there.* I asked to have published professors Charlton Laird and Robert Hume [both older men] added. "What if they should die?" I was told. I think I had mentioned that I'd been hoping to write a Walter Van Tilburg Clark biography for my dissertation, but my committee wants a strictly critical dissertation.

For many reasons I have been seriously thinking of transferring to SUNY Binghamton. Unlike Nevada, Binghamton has a creative writing program and allows students to submit a novel, three-act play or book of short stories for its dissertation requirement. This would satisfy a major interest of mine. Without badmouthing the UNR English Department, SUNY Binghamton has better-known scholars in my opinion. I think I would learn more in Binghamton.

Alice and baby Christian send respectively a hello and a glurp-goo. Fagin stretches a languid paw across the miles to your German shepherd.

Excuse my lack of courtesy in not asking more about Buffalo. I must finish a paper on *King Lear*, noting cannibal imagery in the play.

Sincerely,

Hank

Ed. One of UNR's younger professors Robert Merrill became a well-known Vonnegut and Mailer scholar in the 1990s after Nuwer graduated, but Nuwer did not take a class from Merrill at the time of this letter, though he did later.

1973 The trustees of the State University of New York designated Drew as Buffalo State College's first Distinguished Teaching Professor. Drew's book *John Masefield's England* was published.

Drew's article " A Gift of Books" was published in *The Literary Review*. Drew described English poet Masefield and his American friend Nicholl visiting Manhattan bookshops, where he selected for her reading volumes of poetry by Keats, Housman, Wilde, Yeats, Brooke, Francis Thompson, Moira O'Neill, Tagore, and the first volume of a young American, Archibald MacLeish, his 1917 *Tower of Ivory*.

Nuwer and co-interviewers conducted an interview with visiting author Norman Mailer, later reprinted by Mailer in *The Spooky Art: Some Thoughts on Writing*. Nuwer served as Mailer's chauffeur and later described the experience in his published essay "Driving Mr. Mailer."

9. Nuwer to Drew
University of Nevada
May 19, 1973

Dear Professor Bob:

Thank you very much for your recent letter. I am finished now with grading papers and cramming for three examinations and expect to read a good looking black-jacketed book [by Drew] titled *John Masefield's England*, which Fairleigh Dickinson Press sent me as a review copy. I will first reread Masefield's *Dauber*, *Reynard the Fox*, and some selected short poems to get a better feel for Masefield. I've read nothing of his since reading the two above selections during your class in Contemporary Poetry in 1967.

My completed review will appear in the *Brushfire* literary magazine, which I edit. I'll have another review coming out in the next issue of *Western American Literature* on Pablo Neruda's recent book about a Chilean highwayman in California during the gold fever era.*

I am sorry to hear you are unable to visit Ireland this year. Alice and I hope your father is feeling fine now and that your operation is now forgotten. All is well here but my mother writes that my Dad is missing work again with various ailments. I was hoping to visit Buffalo this summer but that fell through because I was fortunate to get one of the coveted summer school teaching positions open here, and will have preparations to make, and meetings to attend soon.

Therefore, I am packing a bag for Alice and Christian so that they can visit Alice's folks in Newburgh, Brooklyn and eastern New York. I guess she will spend two days in Buffalo too, but I am sure this will entail nothing but hectic visiting obligations for her.

I have been keeping busy. I wrote a three-act play adaptation of Stephen Crane's *The Monster*. I finished a sixth semester German class this year and wrote a paper comparing Richardson's 18th century version of *Aesop's Fables* with Gotthold Ephraim Lessing's translation of 1857. I have a Xerox copy of the former manuscript from the Bodleian Library in Oxford and a typewritten copy of the even rarer German manuscript. At any rate, my professor, Dr. Eugene Grotegut who is chair of the Foreign Language Department, is writing a lengthy article on the textual aspects of the two Fables, and I am writing an opening for his article on Richardson's version.

Grotegut hopes to send it to *Modern Philology* and generously says he will give me co-author status on the article if it is taken by MP. No comparative study has ever been done and only the most cursory examinations of Richardson's version have been made, I am quite excited about doing this study.

Other things I am writing at this time include a note on Poe's "Lenore" and a short story about a boy who contemplates murdering an uncle who senselessly kills two golden eagles and nails them Christlike to the boy's barn to taunt him.

I was awarded a faculty plum given out to one graduate student a semester—the teaching of a freshman honors literature class, which includes material under any theme I wish. I decided to title the course "Black Humor" and will use books by John Barth, Joseph Heller, Kurt Vonnegut, Edward Albee, Bruce Friedman and Anthony Burgess as texts. In addition, I will be getting more money next year: a $450 raise.

I am going to finish this letter here & now before I am forced to write "A Dissertation in Partial etc." at the front of it.

Have a nice summer. My little family says hello. Write if you find time.

Cordially,

Hank

*Ed. Neruda's title was Splendor and Death of Joaquin Murieta.

10. Nuwer to Drew
University of Nevada
October 16, 1973

Dear Professor Bob:

Thank you for your letter of October 8. This really has been an exceptional year for you. I guess that you are waiting for the black and white Buffalo snows to melt so that you can take off for the green shores of Ireland. I must confess that I'd be afraid to travel through Eire while the country is in its current unrest. That recent news episode involving a youth being gunned down while kissing his fiancé good night shocks and saddens me. I've done a bit of reading about Maude Gonne, and I used to be filled with a sort of vicarious excitement over her revolutionary vitality. Now I'm more likely to look upon Gonne with unfriendly eyes. I attended the Catholic seminary in Buffalo, and I can believe, but can't understand, how religion brings out such ungodly barbaric fervor in people.

When you do go to Ireland, Alice and I will worry until you write you're back.

On a cheerier note, the new *Brushfire* is one month from publication. The magazine opens with a lengthy Norman Mailer interview, features poetry by Joyce Carol Oates and Josephine Miles, a review of your book, and a review by Western Literature historian Richard Etulain.

Alice and Christian keep well. Christian at thirteen months already kicks a soccer ball around. Fagin has reluctantly turned over his position in the living room as Cúchulainn of the couch.

Please write whenever you find time. Alice and I are happy when we see the familiar Buffalo State envelope in our mailbox.

Cordially,

Hank

1974 Nuwer and co-interviewer Bill Baines interviewed poets Nikki Giovanni and William Stafford for *Brushfire*. Nuwer earned money by taking assistant editor of the student newspaper *Sagebrush*. He volunteered to put out a newsletter called *The Predator* for the North American Predatory Animal Center, an organization protecting wolves, eagles and coyotes, supported by animal activists Susan St. James, an actress, and Cleveland Amory, a writer and critic.

Drew and Brophy purchased a Doberman they named Lárach, Irish for "little horse." She was gentle and affectionate, but her size and appearance made her an intimidating sight as Drew walked the streets of Tonawanda and Kenmore.

Drew's father died. He was spanked only once by his father—for abusing books at age two by tossing them on the floor. On a walk with his father just before the latter's death in 1974, Drew told him he credited the punishment with instilling a love and respect for books in him. His father merely smiled.

Nuwer's play *Beyond Survival* premiered at the University of Nevada.

11. Nuwer to Drew
University of Nevada
December 8, 1973

Dear Professor Bob:

I received your letter the other day and will respond soon. I am sending *Brushfire* for your use. I wound up in the hospital's emergency room with a stomach ailment, probably colitis, and have been advised to rest. But I'm scheduled to begin rehearsal for a play I'm in, and I'm Graduate School student body president, and so on.

Alice sends her love. How did Buffalo State's soccer team do in 1973?

Best regards,

Hank

12. Nuwer to Drew
University of Nevada
March 2, 1974

Dear Professor Bob:

Hello. I'm afraid this is to be a very brief note. Things are fine here. *Hedda Gabler* ended last week with me in the Lövborg role for a Reno community theatre. I'm in the midst of studying for written exams and editing the *Sagebrush*, *Brushfire* and *The Predator*.

Brushfire's lead article is my interview with National Book Award winner William Stafford of Oregon.

I have another article on teaching composition coming up in a Kansas State publication.

Please drop me a line to let me know how things are in Buffalo. I have been very worried because my father has been in Buffalo's Veterans Hospital since early January. I may have to fly home if things do not improve. Last call my dad seems to be pulling ahead. He had stones removed from his stomach—ironic since half his stomach was removed for gastritis two years ago. I'm afraid the Nuwer stomachs are made from flimsy materials.

Love from all of us,

Hank

13. Nuwer to Drew
University of Nevada
October 26, 1974

Dear Professor Bob:

Things are busy here as usual. I suspect the same is true for you in Buffalo.

I went to Carmel, California a few weeks ago and saw the Robinson Jeffers property from the street, complete with flowers and bulldogs on the premises.

My dog Fagin got into some arsenic-base rat poison under our house. I boarded it up. He nearly died last month. He's fine now but twenty pounds lighter.

Love from the Nuwer family.

Hank

1975 Nuwer's love for biography and the stories behind an author's work instilled in him by Drew collided with the Chicago School of Criticism literary principles of his dissertation adviser Robert Harvey (who had appointed himself head of Nuwer's committee in spite of the student's voiced objections to him).

Nuwer never regretted his decision to attend UNR. Not only did he love his college teaching and the landscape of rural Nevada, but he had formed a friendship with novelist and *National Geographic* staff writer Robert Laxalt. The head of the University of Nevada Press, Laxalt patiently explained to Nuwer that some academic deadlocks could not be resolved—and that Nuwer should just accept the fact and move on to become a writer—advice he took to heart. Nuwer abandoned his studies, out-of-money with student loans due but received Idaho Humanities and National Endowment for the Arts grants to enable him to finish some projects.

In October, Nuwer witnessed two initiations of new pledges by the Sundowners, a local fraternal group of athletes Nuwer knew from intramural sports and student government. They attempted a third initiation miles from campus and pledge John Davies died and a second pledge suffered brain damage, dying years later when a car hit him on a busy Reno street. The shock and sorrow translated into Nuwer's determination to make colleges and high schools report dangerous rites of passage, reflecting his belief that bystanders might save a life if they reported hazing instead of walking away.

Nuwer and wife Alice separated. Nuwer sold a short article to *Esquire*.

14. Nuwer to Drew
University of Nevada
May 8, 1975

Dear Professor Bob:

I wonder if you would consider being one of five people writing a reference for me to the American Conservatory Theatre for a non-academic fellowship from September to May. I would be grateful if you do this. The fellowship provides playwrights with a look into the nuts and bolts of a professional theatre company. Playwrights receive $3,100.

I am one of a few graduate assistants chosen to teach summer school at UNR this summer, which pays me and keeps predator from the door for a few months.

Best,

Hank

15. Nuwer to Drew
University of Nevada
July 15, 1975

Dear Dr. Drew:

Thought you might like to know that I am teaching "Indian Camp" by Ernest Hemingway in composition class today, and that I am using some of the notes you gave our class years back at Buffalo State. I will tell the class about you and read them a section from the Carlos Baker biography on Hemingway, which tells about your adventure in Cuba.

Thanks again for writing that reference for me to the American Conservatory Theatre in San Francisco. Thought you'd be pleased to learn that from all the applicants across the country, I was one of fifteen selected for an interview last week. One of the two interviewers, who is the head of the Squaw Valley [California] Writers' Conference, offered me a full ride to that conference in August. Unfortunately, I had to decline because I am directing a summer camp for mentally retarded people for two weeks in August for the state of Nevada.*

I hope that offer is a sign that I have a good chance to land the ACT playwriting fellowship. The only drawback was that the interviewer said he was worried because I have too many interests. He said he wanted people who have been immersed all their lives in theatre. I gave a feeble response because I could not think of a counterpoint to throw back.

This was the only shaky moment of the interview. My hosts were gracious and kind. I only hope I'm lucky enough to pull one of the three slots.

Please take care of yourself and write when you find time. My Afghan Fagin's coat has grown back after his near-fatal illness last year. He romps about the house like a windup toy.

T'is time to close. Today, *The Predator* goes to bed [the printer] tonight. I also have weightlifting to sweat through. Sometimes I long for Buffalo State when I exercised or played baseball every day.

Best regards,

Hank

*Ed. Nuwer went to the closing of the Squaw Valley conference for writers the day his summer camp duties ended, interviewing poet Galway Kinnell and novelist Herbert Gold. Nuwer's play The Monster *missed an American Conservatory Theatre fellowship but earned a reading by the company in San Francisco. Lacking the money to take an unpaid residency, he turned it down.*

16. Drew to Hank Nuwer
Kenmore, New York
September 30, 1975

Dear Hank,

Having worked as long as I can on this "day off" in my study (I am in the middle of spring scheduling our 50 English professors), and needing a change of pace, I went to the Western American section of my bookshelves (which is now 95 percent Jeffers) and looked for your last letter in my *Brushfires* and other Nuweriana. The most recent one I found is 6 May. Can I have been so long in getting to write back to you? Apparently so.

In the letter I found a carbon of a letter of support for your application to the American Conservatory Theatre in San Francisco. But I doubt that I ever answered your letter.

It was a hot summer for Buffalo. I taught for six weeks, two undergrad surveys of English Nineteenth Century and Irish-English-American early Twentieth Century. Jim, Wolf and I had a week in Vermont, where I deposited most of my Rupert Brooke collection at the University of Vermont for the annual gift to alma mater.

In August, Wolf, who was ten years old on 6 May, became suddenly ill and died on 13 August. Our comfort is that she apparently had no pain during her brief, three-day illness, and the doctors even let us take her home with us for the night before the 13 August surgery during which she died. It was a sudden combination of ruptured spleen and kidney failure and the discovery during surgery of liver cancer. She was buried the following day in a very quiet, attractive pet cemetery in West Seneca with the last four words of Robinson Jeffers's "The House Dog's Grave" on her stone. Jim and I had expected to suffer much grief when her time came but did not dream it would be so bad. This house and its lives were Wolf-centered from morning to night, and we have been just about devastated.

I have two great classes in contemporary literature this fall (the early twentieth century, I mean): they are livelier than usual and both over 35 in size. Next semester I go on sabbatical leave. There is a possibility of going to Tor House for a few days with Donnan and Lee Jeffers, but a seventh Irish jaunt is more likely. Most of the time I expect to be here in Kenmore working, with a short trip to the University of Vermont library the only sure excursion.

The State University of New York is in trouble, along with the State, and New York City and the CUNY [City University of New York], I suppose. We are retrenching and cutting back and all of that, and I am worried even about the retirement pension funds, which the legislature may take to bail New York City out of its billions-bankruptcy-crisis. Locally the department has lost only the two lines occupied by Wilson Gragg and Cleveland Jauch before their deaths this past year, but we may lose more. I am wondering about your degree status, job situation, etc.

Slip me a note when you can.

Love and best wishes to all. Bob

PART II

The Mentor and the Pickup-Truck Journalist

(1976-1984)

17. Nuwer to Drew
Los Angeles
August 17, 1976

Dear Professor Bob:

Hello. Thank you for your kind remarks about my Robinson Jeffers piece and the last *Brushfire* issue. I consider you my mentor and always am overjoyed to hear from you.

You mentioned your own Jeffers's article and that you are looking for a home for it. I spoke to [*Robinson Jeffers Newsletter* editor] Bob Brophy on the telephone the other day and he seems fine. He said he was battling the good fathers of Carmel who are intent on taking over Tor House. They'd climb into Jeffers's grave if they could. No, rest, no rest, even for the dead.

Please send your Jeffers to me because I'd really like to read it. Perhaps you could write and send it to *Western American Literature* at Utah State University. They have accepted five book reviews from me in two years. WAL is a good periodical and I really like reading it. It's never highbrow but informative, contains excellent variation in its criticism—now historical, then archetypal, here traditional—and has allowed me to publish a satirical, decidedly non-scholarly review about Louis L'Amour.

Sorry about some of the bad stuff about Lárach, your pension battle, and neighborhood problems. I hope things have eased up some since your last letter.

Thursday I have dinner with the editor of *Mankind*, a national magazine, which contacted me to write for them. I'm also writing for *Westways*, the AAA magazine; *Coast** and several Los Angeles literary magazines (alas, non-paying). Maybe things are breaking for me finally. Thirty is coming at me like a bolt from Zeus. I've written three screenplays with Gian Carlo Bertelli but with absolutely no luck placing them. I'm still struggling to finish my novel set in Buffalo.

The writing class I'm teaching for UCLA Extension is shaping up. My parents keep well. I'd really like to chat with you after years of correspondence without us meeting. It seems incredible that time has roared by us like this. I had dinner with a Buffalo State alum in Los Angeles who said you were her favorite teacher as well. I hope you know just how much good you have done in your career. I've adopted some of your teaching techniques although I'll never master your calm, unruffled manner.

My regards to Jim Brophy and Henry Sustakoski. Please forgive sloppy typing. I'm tired tonight and rushed.

With best wishes,

Hank

*Ed. The Coast article was an assignment to cover Nuwer's softball game for his Rhino Records team in a double header against Henry Winkler and his Happy Days team at a Hollywood park. Happy Days won the first game with the Fonz pitching and Rhino won the second on a long home run to dead center by Nuwer. The Coast photographer working with Nuwer was a struggling actor named Ed Begley, Jr.

1976 Nuwer accepted an offer from Italian screenwriter Gian-Carlo Bertelli, past-president of Reno-based Lear Jets owned by his father-in-law, to go to Los Angeles to co-write screenplays. The offer was extended following a dinner at the home of Gian Carlo and Shanda Lear Bertelli with Bill and Moira Lear, owners of the Lear jet empire.

Nuwer, his son Chris, and his dog Fagin lived out of his 1959 Chevy Apache van for nearly three months on Los Angeles beaches while co-writing with Bertelli three unproduced screenplays. Bertelli later moved to homes in Italy and Switzerland to write The *Secret Life of Sergei Eisenstein* and a number of successful screenplays and documentaries.

Nuwer worked in a daycare for three hours a day so that son Chris could play there safely while Nuwer wrote the screenplays with Bertelli (Chris stayed some nights with Bertelli and his then-wife Shanda, while Nuwer slept on a Santa Monica beach in his van.). Nuwer formed a lifelong friendship with daycare worker Margie Robinson, then a graduate student at Long Beach State, who later resurfaced in an important way in 2006.

One of the freelance articles Nuwer was assigned was from *Mankind*, a nationally known history publication, to write a feature on Robinson Jeffers and his famed stone Hawk Tower in Carmel, California. Nuwer brought along his son Christian who mischievously hid in Hawk Tower. Jeffers' son Donnan was amused, saying that generations of Jeffers children had done the same thing. *Mankind* folded with Nuwer's article at press.

Nuwer formed friendships or acquaintances with many book and magazine writers, including Carole Mallory (destined to gain infamy as mistress to Mailer), Nick Tosches, Lester Bangs, Barry Farrell, David Harrison, Ben Pesta, Emmett Grogan, Richard Melzer, Joe Nick Patoski, and Buffalo native Toyomi Igus, later to become the recipient of the 2004 Western New York Women's Hall of Fame Award.

Alice and Nuwer reconciled for a brief time in Los Angeles.

1977 Nuwer and wife Alice separated again and moved toward an amicable divorce, agreeing to work together to give son Christian a good life. Nuwer moved to Topanga Canyon in California, taking the place of a tenant who apparently had been a friend of actress Tippi Hendren's daughter, Melanie Griffith, then 20. Shortly after moving into the cabin he came home one evening to find the young star of the movie *Night Moves* asleep in his bed like Goldilocks in the fairy tale. When Nuwer explained he now lived in this cabin, Melanie Griffith shrugged, dressed, and left.

1978 Nuwer lost touch with family and friends such as Drew as he crossed and re-crossed the United States and Mexico many times in his capacity as a struggling freelance writer. Summers, holidays, and some weekends his young son Chris joined him on the road and even accompanied him as he conducted interviews for magazines.

Nuwer wrote dozens of stories for *New West, Rocky Mountain, Country Gentleman, Gentlemen's Quarterly,* Buffalo *Courier-Express Sunday Magazine, The Saturday Evening Post, Writer's Digest,* and other magazines, but barely met expenses some months. He wrote an extensive piece on hazing deaths and the psychology of hazing for *Human Behavior* magazine, interviewing experts in behavior such as Buffalo-born Irving Janis, author of the Groupthink theory, and Lionel Tiger, author of *Men in Groups.*

1979 In the *American Book Collector,* Drew wrote a piece on Thornton Wilder and his correspondence with him.

Nuwer's Buick died in New Mexico while covering a horse race at Ruidoso, and he bought an ancient GMC pickup. He appeared on Tom Snyder's *Tomorrow Show* on national television in February with Snyder dubbing him the "Pickup Truck Journalist." Accompanying Nuwer in the studio was close friend David Harrison and his girlfriend, actress and Berlin lead vocalist Terri Nunn.

Nuwer traveled to Minnesota, interviewing farmers and power co-op executives. Farmers had been protesting a power line built on their farmland and turned violent, destroying towers and other equipment. Nuwer's editors on the Minnesota story were Kai Bird (later a successful author) at *The Nation*, and Anita Shreve at *Us*, destined to become a best-selling novelist.

At the request of well-known editor Bob Gleason, Nuwer created a potboiler series of novels called *The Bounty Hunter*, co-written with a former biker and sometimes skip tracer William (Tiny) Boyles. The books provided an income at last, but Nuwer hated writing them, although he loved hearing the colorful tales Boyles told for the book—many tall and some true. He worked on his "serious" novel, a satire of graduate school Ph.D. programs that was set in Buffalo and in Nevada.

He continued his travels all over the United States and Mexico on story assignments in the pickup with acclaimed photographer Max Aguilera-Hellweg, a former *Rolling Stone* photographer. He wrote three profiles of Olympic legend Al Oerter and became lifelong friends with Oerter's wife, the former long jumper Cathy Carroll, and attended the couple's wedding on a boat in Long Island Sound.

Nuwer worked with California junkyard owner and millionaire filmmaker H.B. (Toby) Halicki on the latter's new screenplay through an introduction from Boyles, an actor in Halicki's movie *Gone in 60 Seconds*.

Nuwer chanced to run into romance author and Miss Universe judge Rosemary Rogers whom he once had profiled for *Writer's Digest*, and the two dated through 1981. Her rigorous work habits and advice she gave him on self-editing and rewriting were lifelong work lessons for him as a book author. Francesco Scavullo included a portrait of Rogers in his book *Beautiful Women*.

1980 Toby Halicki refused to give Nuwer full credit on the partially completed screenplay, offering a researcher credit only. The two men refused to compromise and parted business company, but stayed friends. *The Junkman* later was made and released to poor reviews.

Nuwer conducted dozens of magazine interviews for stories, often accompanied by photographers such as Max Aguilera Hellweg. In Idaho Nuwer and Aguilera-Hellweg flew in an old Beaver plane with two back-country pilots above River-of-No-Return country in Idaho on assignment for *Rocky Mountain* magazine, edited by Robert (Bob) Wallace, who coached Hank by phone and offered writing tips on creating scenes in nonfiction. One of the two pilots died in a plane crash right after the issue went on the stands. Nuwer and Aguilera-Hellweg also visited a Crow reservation in Montana to do a serious piece on the Native American tribe and its ways for *Country Gentleman* magazine.

In a profile of Hank Nuwer published by the Buffalo *Courier-Express*, Nuwer discussed the influence of Professor Fraser Drew on his career.

18. Drew to Hank Nuwer, c/o Halicki Studios
Danbury Lane, Kenmore, New York
15 June 1980

Dear Hank,

You have been wandering in and out of my mind for some time now. In fact a letter sent to you several months ago…came back from an old address I now forget. This morning I was looking at the Buffalo *Courier-Express* and had finished the sports section when the cover of the *Sunday Magazine* caught my eye with its picture of Buffalo, Kansas. I turned to the article and suddenly caught your name, then the picture of you and Christian, and then my own name. Starting over, I read the piece with great interest, especially the account of what you have been doing and writing. This is all tremendous!

It would be hard to tell you how proud of what you *are* and what you are *doing* without getting sticky. Perhaps later, when I have come down off this sudden news feature a bit. And when I have stopped congratulating myself for what you told the article-writer about me, and my influence on you. That was a generous thing to do, and the pleasure I take in your doing it will never diminish. One comment like that, however unjustified, from someone like you can justify a whole lifetime of teaching. I'll stop at this point on that subject.

I keep the things that you have sent to me, and the pictures, and I like very much the one of you and your son in the paper. It is a great thing for you both that you could travel together this summer. This afternoon, by chance, I saw *Kramer vs. Kramer* and, sentimental bachelor that I am, was moved out of control by the relationship of the father and young son in that film.

The nearest relationship I have had to father-son began in the fall of 1977, when a freshman geology major showed up in my contemporary literature class in his first semester with a crowd of upperclassmen. I liked the look and sound of him when I tried to "counsel him out" of the class and let him stay. He got the top grade in a fast class and has been with me every semester since, thanks to an independent study set-up we now have. A year ago now he and I were in Ireland on my first trip "home" in seven years and my seventh trip.

Tom [Hoar] stayed on [in] Europe for the summer in Ireland and the fall in the Hebrides, France (grape-picking), Italy, and Austria, coming home for Christmas and second semester. He had talked me into going [to Ireland] via sleeping bag and tent with no schedule. We were 66 and 20 instead of the 33 and seven of you and Christian, but it was a rejuvenation for me.

I am teaching a short-course seminar in Modern Ireland this summer and then relaxing for the rest of it.

Here is a laugh for you. I wrote my first five poems after coming back from Ireland, and the first one, first in my whole damned life of living on the edges of poetry, I sold to an illustrated Dublin magazine, *Ireland of the Welcome*s; the second was taken by *Housman Journal* in England. I haven't had the nerve to send the others anywhere; they are all pretty bad—local, adjectival. But I had another feeling of getting out of my rut, as in the camping in Ireland.

Regards,

Bob

18. Nuwer to Drew
Short-term rental cabin in Idyllwild, California
June 30, 1980

Dear Professor Bob:

Quick note this time because I'm in the midst of book and magazine deadlines. I promise to write a longer letter soon.

Thanks for your generous words and copy of your article. I'm envious of the Ireland trip. My own life proceeds from assignment to assignment. Unfortunately, unless your name is Uris, Ireland pieces from magazines usually go to American writes already living abroad.

In less than four weeks I'm off for Wyoming to finish a piece on female herders. I have pieces out this month in *Country Gentleman* on Basque herders in Nevada and in the *Saturday Evening Post* (as I have had for six straight issues) on a sports figure. Oh, yes, I also have a piece on historical novelist Rosemary Rogers finally coming out in *Writer's Yearbook*.

Glad you saw the *Courier* piece and even happier you wrote. I still have the Robert Frost picture and signed Louise Nicholl book. I promise to stay closer in touch. I'm finishing another [Bounty Hunter] adventure novel due to my editor in October.

Hope your health is excellent. You look rugged as a Druid in the picture. I have a small rental cabin here with Christian for the summer. It is glorious out here.

Warmly,

Hank

19. Nuwer to Drew
Halicki Studios, Los Angeles
October 3, 1980

Dear Professor Bob:

Quick note to stay in touch. I'll be on the road once again to write in a few hours, this time until June 1981. [Attached is address of *Denver Magazine*, my next stop]. I'll be in Buffalo in January. Hope the teaching and your projects go well. I've decided not to spend a semester teaching for Antioch West [which had offered Nuwer a part-time position at its Idylwild campus in California]. There is an itch that sends me on the road.

Take care,

Hank

1981 Louise Townsend Nicholl died. Drew's 1,046 letters from Nicholl were placed in the Fraser Drew collection of Masefield at Bailey/Howe Library at UVM.

Nuwer earned enough on the last road trip to buy a barely used Datsun pickup truck with camper and moved into a tiny apartment in a former monastery in the Hollywood Hills. Nuwer took daily breaks from the book in January to take hundreds of ground balls hit him by friend Ben Pesta, an attorney, editor and Air Force veteran, so he could be in shape to spend a week of spring training in Florida, playing first base on *Denver Magazine* and *Courier-Express* assignments for the Montreal Expos minor league organization managed by Felipe Alou and Jim

Fanning. He played in two games and numerous practice games and sessions. Max Aguilera Hellweg captured all on film.

Later in year, he stopped in Buffalo to see his folks and met Drew by appointment at Buffalo State College, interviewing him for the Buffalo *Courier-Express*. Late in the year, he left the road and began caretaking a tiny wilderness cabin in Berry Creek, California, purchasing, breaking and training a horse named Surprise. (The former owner had purchased a mare, not knowing she was pregnant with this filly—hence the name).

Nuwer and co-author Carole Shaw, editor and publisher of BBW [*Big Beautiful Woman*] magazine, completed a book called *Come Out, Come Out, Wherever You Are*, a book for plus-sized women that covered such issues as job discrimination. The book contained interviews with ordinary women and celebrities such as Dionne Warwick and introduced Nuwer to feminist theories. *Ms. Magazine* in 1982 gave the book a positive review.

20. Nuwer to Drew
Berry Creek, California
October 10, 1981

Dear Professor Bob:

I started three letters to you the past two months, but this one I promise is actually going to get mailed.

First of all, how are you? It was delightful meeting you again after all those years. Believe me, I went away from our chat buzzing with enthusiasm about writing and delightfully buzzing with the glow of the Irish whiskey, too. Christian loved his dolphin [gift], and he promises to write a thank you note. It's hard to get him over writing blocks he gets when asked to produce literary masterpieces and thank you notes.

My life situation is changing, and I am a bit apprehensive though excited. Jenine Howard, a lovely lady who used to be an editor at the *Saturday Evening Post* and *Country Gentleman*, is moving out here to the wilderness to live with me.

Which brings me to my residence. Tor House it ain't, nor your wonderful home, either, but it is a delightful forest sanctuary deep in the wilderness, which permits me to write without fear of duns looking over my shoulder as Herman Melville used to complain. I have a two-room A-frame (one up and one down) in which I have some of the amenities: a stove, fridge and furniture. I rely on a chamber pot, and I must truck in my water. I bought a pretty quarter horse, a three-year old named Surprise, and I take my showers at the place she is pastured.

You would not believe how gorgeous the ridges are here. Yesterday I took a drive in the late afternoon past big oaks heavy with mistletoe, their leaves red, yellow and orange, and set against a backdrop of pretty sugar pines and tenacious Manzanita. There also are several madrone trees here, too.

My good news is that because I am now living so economically (dirt poor!), I am finally able to give full attention to my novel, *Shuffle Off to Buffalo*. It opens with a "So There" to novelist and critic Frank Norris who wrote that a good novel could never be set in Buffalo.

I had a wonderful interview with Maurice Sendak, the artist who does such wonderful books for kids. I'm enclosing that piece. He was an inspiration, and we've chatted by phone since. We share a mutual love for Melville, mutts and Mozart.

Say hi to Jim Brophy for me. Thanks for opening your home last visit.

Warmly,

Hank

21. Drew to Nuwer
Buffalo State College
18 November 1981*

Dear Hank,

I had been thinking about you but had mislaid the letter on which you wrote several phone numbers and addresses [while on the road]. Now I have your Berry Creek address. I am in my office now and may not get very far with this letter, but at least I'll begin.

I didn't get very far. Students began arriving with various problems and the day disappeared. Today is free of classes, conferences and meetings and so I may be able to get some kind of a letter off to you.

I am glad that you enjoyed our reunion. I certainly did. It was fine to sit down with you in the office at the college and at home among the books.

I think it is great that Jenine is coming out to share your corner of the wilderness, and the country and the A-frame sound fine. And a horse. The whole set-up sounds ideal, and I think that you will get some work done there along with clean air and basic good living.

Tell Christian not to worry about a thank-you note. Jim says it is enough that he liked the dolphin gift.

Speaking of gifts, that was a great package you sent. I have already read the article about JaVoan Brantner [female sheepherder in remote Idaho] and the interview with Maurice Sendak. I liked them both tremendously and marvel at your ability to get so far into two such diverse people and situations. The Montreal Expos picture of you pleased me very much. I took it to school to show to Courter and Sustakoski and did find Eloise, who was pleased to see it. Marvin LaHood and Carole Brown, my good friends in the department, were much impressed. Marvin said, "Jesus, he looks like the real thing [at bat]!" I assured him that you were.

The Christmas gift of the first draft of the novel is, as you knew, right on the line for a collector and a Nuwer fan. Over the coming holiday I will enjoy reading it, after which it will join books, articles, letters, pictures on the Hank-shelf which is close to the Jeffers-shelf.

That was a fine package to receive and just at a time when I could use a lift. My friend-since-1948, Louise Townsend Nicholl, died on 11 November in a New Jersey nursing home. Her doctor had phoned her lifelong friend Irene Nunemaker [philanthropist and sometimes writer] in Kansas and Irene at once wrote me. I was grateful for the news, for Louise was about ninety and had been completely out of it for several years, not recognizing anyone and unable to read or write. But I was grieving for the Louise that had been, and your letter and package lifted spirits greatly.

Yours, Bob

*Ed. Drew put down the letter and picked it up and re-dated it 19 November 1981.

1982 In January Nuwer learned that the rented cabin was to be sold. Nuwer gave away his horse and relocated to South Carolina, where he had writing assignments. Nuwer interviewed poet James Dickey, author John Jakes and other notables in South Carolina, while Jenine snapped photographs. Jenine on her own shot freelance photographs of a Buffalo marine for the Buffalo *Courier-Express* at Parris Island. Nuwer left the couple's temporary home in Beaufort to go on the road to research several articles in Florida, interviewing the owners of the champion horse Timely Writer and major leaguers Pete Rose, Jim Kaat, Woody Fryman, and many others. Nuwer sat one game with former Red Sox slugger Ted Williams in stands cordoned off for the press and talked baseball all game.

Nuwer and Jenine Howard married in April after he finished a rewrite for *Boston Magazine* on Timely Writer. He had fifteen minutes to spare for a shower and then the couple made a mad dash to get to the church on time. The couple learned on April 15 that Hank was a finalist for a position teaching journalism at Clemson University. A grammarian and editor, Jenine Nuwer was an important influence on Nuwer's writing craft.

At Clemson, Nuwer invited contacts such as photographer Max Aguilera Hellweg and World War Two spy-turned-author Richard Dunlop to speak to the student body. He himself lectured at a scholarly conference in Atlanta, where James Dickey was speaking. Nuwer gave a talk at a session on humor writing with authors Roy Blount, William Price Fox and Lewis Grizzard.

Late in year in 1982, on Nuwer's visit to his ill father in Buffalo, he and BSC friend Joe Nikiel were Buffalo *Courier-Express* guests at the farewell party for the paper.

22. Drew to Nuwer
Ontario, Canada
10 January 1982

First of all, Happy New Year to you, Chris and Jenine!

I was pleased with your card and with the message that the *Courier* was going to print your article. Then, last Monday Mitch Gerber [a Buffalo *Courier-Express* staff editor] called and we made [an] appointment for me with the photographer at the office at Buffalo State for Tuesday morning. Gerber, who seemed very pleasant, asked me to bring an earlier photograph of myself and the picture with Éamon de Valera.

I liked the photographer, who engaged me in conversation and then snapped pictures. Since I have given up cigarettes and never had a pipe for more than a week, he had to use a book as a prop. He thought that the somewhat faded color print of Jim, de Valera and me in the President's study in Dublin would do. He also took along one of me in brush cut (!) descending from an Aer Lingus jet at Shannon in 1967, and one of SUNY Chancellor [Ernest] Boyer presenting me with a medal emblematic of the first Distinguished Teaching Professorship in 1973...Sorry I did not have one taken with Hemingway. However, the photographer took one of a Christmas card inscribed to me by Ernest Hemingway. Then he placed three Ernest Hemingway letters together, fan-shaped, and I suggested a photo of Hemingway superimposed on the letters (thus covering enough of the letters to comply with the copyright restrictions on Ernest Hemingway letters). Enough of these should come out to disfigure your text.

Naturally, I am very eager to see what you wrote...Cold as hell here and snowy. I hope that you made out all right with that California weather. One report had seven feet of snow in the mountains. Berry Creek? If you were there, I hope you had plenty of firewood and firewater and pemmican.

It is -7 here and wind gusts and spitting snow make it seem like -27. I go back to school on the 18 [of January]. Meanwhile, good luck in your work and your weather.

Best to all three.

Bob

23. Nuwer to Drew
Beaufort, South Carolina
April 16, 1982

Dear Professor Bob:

I've owed a letter for so long I wonder where to begin.

First of all, thank you so much for the recommendation. I am waiting for acceptance or rejection from Clemson's English Department. The interviews, I believe, went well. Over 25 people—including the Dean, chair and search committee—interviewed me. In a couple cases, "interrogated" me might be the accurate term. Essentially, as I understand it, the department must decide whether it wants a man with practical experience (me) or someone with a Ph.D. (Mr. X).

If your ears were burning last Monday, it might be because the committee asked me how I first came to want to write. I told them all about you at length. They were impressed with the way you went after interviews with Frost and Hemingway with gusto.

Jenine and I were married two weeks ago. Chris flew in for the occasion: a lovely and glorious time was had by our trio.

I miss Berry Creek, California, and the remote cabin. But we were going to be dumped out in the woods any moment since the owner of the A-frame had placed the A-frame and property up for sale.

This address in South Carolina is temporary. I take on a dozen magazine articles between now and May 23. Thus, I have other irons in the fire, but none so attractive as a tenure-track assistant professorship requiring but a nine-hour semester teaching load. Since I am concentrating on good work more and more, I would like to teach while turning out short stories and "New Journalism" pieces. I have vowed never to write another "Bounty Hunter" book again. It is just too hard on my psyche every time I enter a bookstore and see someone like Pat Conroy (age 27) turning out wonderful fiction. In other words, my loyal and dear mentor, the time has come to make my stand.

At this time I wish we were sitting down over a whiskey and talking over dreams and books. I shudder to think how I probably would be working in an ad agency or maybe far worse if you hadn't offered assistance to an eager, unlettered kid fifteen years ago who dropped his creative writing on your desk and said, "Here, what do you think?"

Well, I'll close. I'll let you know if the position materializes. Who knows, there just might be a kid in class that will need a nudge in the direction of his or her life's dreams.

Let me know if there is anything I can do for you or your students.

Warmly,

Hank

24. Drew to Nuwer
Kenmore, New York
23 April 1982

Dear Hank,

First things first: congratulations on your marriage!!! I am very happy for you both. Give Jenine my love.

Now to other matters. When I got home from a vacation out West to Wyoming, just before midnight, Jim told me of your call and gave me the address of the Clemson University English chairman. I got off a mailgram before midnight. I had hoped Dr. M. Thomas Inge would get in touch with me for more detailed information as I suggested, but perhaps it was not necessary. Anyhow, I hope that you got the job if it seemed right for you.

Wyoming was great. I loved what I saw of the big, windy state. I would have seen more except that I did not adjust quickly to the altitude. Doctor here told me to stay under 8,000 feet. The day I thought I would be going over a 9,600 foot pass to Jackson and the Tetons, I was panting and puffing at 6,000.

Love, Bob

25. Drew to Nuwer
Kenmore, New York
27 April 1982

Dear Hank,

It isn't often that you can write a guy two congratulatory letters in three days. April 1982 will go down in history for you as Jenine and Clemson month.

The phone call last night did me a tremendous amount of good…the news itself, of course, first of all, but also the fact that you would call and tell me. I could not be happier for you.

Now you have an academic base from which to operate. You'll have the options of a virtually academic commitment or any kind of mix of teaching and writing which you may work out. Your comments about burn-out were interesting. In any event, it was time for some kind of change and this looks like a good one. You will always be a writer and a good one. You will also like teaching and be a good teacher. Maybe they will balance. Or you may turn out to be a great writer who keeps one foot in the teaching world…Frost always did.

I have much respect for Clemson, although I do not know much about it. And it is more than a hangover from my years at another ACC school, Duke. I have a cousin, not first, maybe third, Jeanne Fraser MacDonald of Anderson, the widow of George R. McDonald, who must be a rich woman. She and her late husband established a scholarship fund at Clemson. I have never met here but have exchanged a dozen letters with her in the past several years. She is on the Scots side of the family, not the Irish…I have other friends in Columbia, a retired Air Force colonel and his wife. Edward Tokaz ("Tik") was my good friend in the middle and late 1930s, and I have stayed in touch with him all these years, although our physical paths have not crossed since 1940. He was a Massachusetts native but married a South Carolina girl.

Back to Clemson again. The nine-hour load is great, too. Our English professors all teach twelve, including two sections of freshman composition, except for Henry Sustakoski who now does the schedules, John Reedy who chairs freshman comp, and Distinguished Service Professor [J. Stephen] Sherwin and Distinguished Teaching Professor Drew. Nine hours is a civilized load. By the way, did you know that our English Department has two of the College's three [SUNY] Distinguished ranks? The third is Joe Wincenc of Music, who got the same rank as I have about four years ago.

You will like the students, almost all of them, and you will find one to nudge now and then. I have the feeling that they will find *you*. Most of the work will be fun, some of it exciting, and the rewards are tremendous. Now and then there will be a great colleague. And some of your students will turn into friends. Take out of my own life the friends who have come out of the college classroom and it would be a poor life. I can count you and Tom [Hoar] and Jim Brophy and Jini Rizzo, Bea Beckman, for examples. Jini graduated in 1948, and 34 years and her seven kids later we still get together every few weeks for lunch.

Check in when you can.

Bob

PS: I think it was terrific that Christian came on for the wedding.

26. Nuwer to Drew
Clemson, South Carolina
September 15, 1982

Dear Professor Bob:

Midnight. Two stacks of papers await me before 9 a.m. class. Just a quick note to let you know the *Courier* is planning to run a much shorter version of my piece on you. I'm disappointed, but with the much-lamented demise of the *Courier* ahead, I feared the piece would miss print entirely. At least this way, some of my words about you will find their way to your colleagues' breakfast table.

The teaching goes very well. My writing continues. The fourth Bounty Hunter book is out now, along with a hardcover book for large women that I wrote with TV personality Carole Shaw. Recent articles of mine appeared in *Boston, Carolina Lifestyle, Saturday Evening Post* (two), and others. I hope to show the Clemson folk they didn't hire a deadhead. Please send me one issue of the *Courier* for my records. I'm sure Mitch Gerber is too busy job hunting to remember a trivial matter.

All best,

Hank

27. Drew to Nuwer
Kenmore, New York
15 September 1982

Dear Hank,

This afternoon I called Mitch Gerber from the college to thank him for the fine presentation of your article in today's paper. As you have probably heard (he said he called you a few days ago), the *Courier-Express* is in deep trouble and may not survive past 19 September. Mitch seemed very pessimistic about its chances and the finding of a satisfactory buyer. He is busy tying up loose ends and asked me if I would send you a copy of the appropriate pages.

And so here they are. I am delighted with the article. You may have gilded this lily, says he with becoming modesty, but I sure like the way you did it. I have been very tired lately. Your article, and especially its appearance just under the wire of the paper's probable closing, is a real shot in the arm and I am doubly grateful for it. While I cannot speak with any grace about your subject matter, I certainly like the way you handled it (him) and your beginning and end and the whole atmosphere of the piece.

I am pleased that so many of the pictures were used, and I like the one on page 5 that the *Courier* photographer took. If the paper were not in such a state, I would try hard to get a glossy of that for posterity and my personal rogue's gallery.

I am into the new semester with what you called a bumper crop in both sections of Contemporary Lit, more in freshman writing than I'd choose, and a few good independent studies.

We'll be in touch. And my thanks again, and very best wishes.

Bob

28. Drew to Nuwer

Kenmore, New York

3 October 1982

Dear Hank and Jenine,

A quick one today. I just bought the one book I've always wanted most, even more than the rare Hemingways and Jeffers—a first edition of Housman's *A Shropshire Lad*. I got it from an English dealer for £510, under $900, a good price. I've been stroking it affectionately. It's a nice companion to the first of Robert Frost's *A Boy's Will* and the first editions of first books of Hemingway, Jeffers, William Faulkner, W.B. Yeats, T.S. Eliot, Thornton Wilder, Thomas Wolfe, Hart Crane and Masefield. But now my book buying is over.

Housman is a poet for adolescents and nostalgic old men, but he's been my man all the way from one extreme to the other.

Love, Bob

29. Drew to Nuwer

Clemson, South Carolina

October 13, 1982

Dear Professor Bob:

Wholly inadequate mail for you, but enjoy this postcard of Carl Sandburg's study at Connemara Farms in Flat Rock, North Carolina, where we petted goats and scoped out Carl's library.

Here is a dismal attempt to stay in better touch. I have four more articles to research but my stack of papers to grade never recedes. Every time I grade a group and reach for my own work, a fresh stack of student papers or a professor request to read his work appears on my desk.

I remind me of Tantalus, reaching for writing time instead of food and water!

Warmly,

Hank

30. Nuwer to Drew
Clemson, South Carolina
Turkey Day, November 1982

Dear Professor Bob:

Enclosed please find a few recent clips. I have been really enjoying lecturing a little more though it doesn't come easy for me, and I get butterflies.

All is well and no. My student evaluations and department evaluations are excellent. But Jenine's editing talents are going to waste. Unless she can find a job, we can't afford to stay here financially, and Clemson cannot have me back for 1983-1984. I can freelance wherever she goes to work, but the reverse is clearly not true.

How is your health? Retirement closer?

Heard from Mitch Gerber, ex-*Courier-Express* editor. He landed at the *Orlando Sentinel*. Thought you might like to know.

Since Thanksgiving is a time of truly giving thanks, I want to do just that. Thanks for all your love and support over the last 15 years, Professor Bob. Hi to Jim.

Warmly,

Hank

31. Nuwer to Drew
Clemson, South Carolina
December 18, 1983

Dear Professor Bob:

Christmas greetings.

I have a grant to study the full manuscript of Hemingway's *The Dangerous Summer* at the John F. Kennedy library near Boston. For Christmas son Chris flies into Atlanta on Monday.

Warmly,

Hank

1983 Fraser Drew retired from Buffalo State College on July 1. One of his gifts to BSC Special Collections was his small but valuable Langston Hughes (1902-1967) letter collection (including treasured letters from Hughes to Drew) and first editions such as *The Weary Blues* in memory of Dean Ralph Horn. He also donated signed John Masefield books in memory of Dr. Rockwell and others. His articles on scholarship and teaching totaled 194 in his career.

Brophy and Drew lost Lárach at age eight from a heart attack, purchasing a miniature pinscher they named Sugar and another Drew called Sionnach, Irish for "fox." Sionnach liked to burrow in Drew's sweater to go to sleep, a practice she often repeated with startled visitors to the house.

Nuwer learned he has erred in renting a huge, expensive house from a professor on sabbatical. He struggled to pay bills on the small teaching salary but resolutely refused to write any more potboilers or accept assignments from magazines he does not respect, turning down several offers. His confidence eroded as his novel kept collecting letters of rejection and unsigned rejection slips.

After the sabbatical house contract ended, Nuwer looked for a rental house he can afford on his low $21,000 salary. The only one he could find that he can afford chokes him with the scent of cat urine and is uninhabitable by any standards. When Clemson announced a salary freeze, Nuwer reluctantly resigned from Clemson but continued to write for its journal, the *South Carolina Review*.

Jenine later in year accepted work as a senior editor in Idaho for *Satellite Orbit* magazine, and they relocated again. In the summer before leaving, they attended the Long Island Sound wedding of Hank's old friends, discus thrower Al Oerter and long jumper Cathy Carroll, and took a quick side trip to Buffalo for relatives and Jenine's first meeting with Fraser Drew.

32. Nuwer to Drew
Clemson, South Carolina
February 14, 1983

Dear Professor Bob:

Just a quick note to make sure all is well with you. I have finished a short story I've been meaning to share with you, but I think I'll let it sit a month to see if it holds up to rereading.

Perhaps you may get to meet Jenine before the summer is out. I would like that very much.

The university apparently likes my work. My reviews were excellent, and I was able to publish 15 articles last semester. However, I won't be satisfied until I am turning out quality fiction. This short story is an important step for me.

I'll close. Too many papers to correct tonight, alas.

My dad continues to weaken. If my budget permits, I'll fly up one weekend.

The new *Atlantic Magazine* National Affairs editor Gregg Easterbrook is from Kenmore West High originally. We chatted briefly last week by phone (and we know some of the same faculty*, but he and I never have met personally). He is a smart writer, good on analysis, and I predict a great career for him.

With all good wishes,

Hank

Ed. Nuwer had performed his student teaching at Kenmore West in 1968.

33. Drew to Nuwer
Kenmore, New York
17 February, 1983

Dear Hank,

I haven't been very good at writing to you, either, for similar reasons to yours, and so your letter, which came now calls for an immediate reply, such as it may be. You guys have been on my mind quite a bit, however, when I have had a chance to think about people who are important to me. I have been wondering about your directions and destinations, sure always that the traveling would be interesting and productive wherever it leads.

Love,

Bob

34. Nuwer to Drew
Randolph, Vermont
July 22, 1983

Dear Professor Bob:

Greetings from your old haunts. Just was at *Yankee Magazine* to show my portfolio and maybe kick up an assignment for an article or two. Jenine and I will get to Buffalo this summer.

Love,

Hank

35. Drew to Hank Nuwer
Kenmore, New York
27 August 1983

Dear Hank and Jenine,

It is good that you saw the back of this place when you did. We finally yielded to the voice of good sense and had the two giant willows taken down; a huge branch, perfectly healthy, had come down on a quiet evening, and we remembered how we dreaded winds and ice storms. The trees were very old and had been held together in part by cables. They went down this week and all the other trees—ash, maple, tulip, elm—were trimmed of dead wood. Jim took Lárach and me to Canada to avoid the noise and activity for three days.

The yard no longer looks like a quiet park, and on warm evenings I shall miss the plantation-like look of the weeping branches. Now there is lots of sky and electric wires show. We go tomorrow night to see about replacement trees like ash, locust, linden, and silver and sugar maples.

It is good that you were here...and I greatly enjoyed seeing Hank again and meeting Jenine. As your note said, it was as if we had met often before. I also loved your strawberry hat, but don't feel you must wear it if you come next in midwinter, Jenine. Your hat was very sharp, too, Hank.

I suppose that the biggest non-willow news since your visit is that the administration has denied my request to teach a section of contemporary lit or Irish [lit] in the fall. I think with shameless immodesty that the college is missing out on a bargain. I would teach free if the union permitted and was willing to take $1,200, the price of a graduate assistant for [one] section of freshman composition. Registration occurs next week, and I plan to go in and see any of my students who are on the premises and a few selected colleagues. If I encounter my dean, I shall tell him how attractive his presence makes my retirement. As I surely told you, the SUNY distinguished rank entitles me to keep my office, and I intend to make some use of it...Meanwhile, there will be books to read and perhaps something to write and places to see and ex-baseball-playing students who write well and marry beautiful editors to keep in touch with (elegant sentence, that). There will also be the joy of staying inside on foul mornings. This year's trip is planned for Wyoming in November...

I learned a few things from reading *The Hemingway Women**, particularly the fact that Martha Gellhorn was not all bad and that Mary Hemingway is more or less incommunicado. I had no Christmas card from her in '81 or '82.

Time to get myself scoured and accoutered for a dinner at the Cloister this evening in belated celebration of Jim's birthday. It should be fun. The hostess, a spry lady of advanced years and an addiction to someone's book of synonyms, is a favorite of us both, and we love her conversation.

Hey, Jenine, you don't have to call me "Professor" Anybody. Hank's memory of the classroom makes "Bob" difficult for him, but don't let him live with inhibition or pass it on to you. The flowers remained beautiful for several days in spite of our guests' breathy admiration that evening [that they were] outshining their Waterford vase from County Waterford. Thank you both again.

Report in when you can. Have fun with that new house. Have fun period. Hugs, greetings from all here.

Bob

*Ed: a present from Hank and Jenine to Drew, along with a bouquet of flowers.

36. Nuwer to Drew
Auburn, Alabama
Undated, circa October 1, 1983

Dear Professor Bob:

Hope this note finds you well.

Another note on the run. Just finished researching an *Inside Sports* article on Auburn Coach Pat Dye and Bo Jackson and Tigers football and headed back to Bloomington to write the sucker—6,000 words. Lots of humorous tales to insert in this one. Look for it at newsstands around December 4.

Jenine and I soon will head for Oklahoma to profile basketball star Wayman Tisdale and Coach Billy Tubbs in Norman, then down to Lafayette, Louisiana for me to spend another week interviewing Yankees Ragin' Cajun pitcher Ron Guidry and his family. Both of these are for *Inside Sports*, and I am a contributing writer on the masthead.

Mainly I am attaching a couple pictures of you, Jenine and me from the reunion we had at your house last summer. The fun we had seems to shine in all our faces.

The weather has been marvelous. We are looking forward to Nevada visit at Christmas to see son Chris.

Best, Hank

37. Nuwer to Drew
Bloomington, Indiana
Labor Day, 1983

Dear Professor Bob:

Just a note of thanks to you and Jim for the terrific lunch and your thoughtful wedding gift. It has been a fruitful August and early

September for I have been assigned considerable freelance work. Chris, Jenine and I have managed to fish and play a lot on nearby lakes.

Warmly,

Hank

38. Nuwer to Drew
Bloomington, Indiana
November 27, 1983

Dear Professor Bob:

Just came back from Louisiana and must head to Chicago for *Saturday Review* soon. Jenine and I spent Thanksgiving in a Ramada Inn in Jackson, Mississippi, scarfing down rubbery turkey after driving 450 miles that day. So many magazines pay on publication, instead of acceptance, that despite a backlog of over $10,000 due me, I'm forced to borrow from the bank to meet expenses.

We had a ghastly experience. I came back from the trip to find that a ten-day feeder had horribly fouled my fish tank. I changed the water, using our cistern water which is supposedly pure. I don't know what chemical was in the water, or what oxygen was missing in that water, but the fish literally choked to death—gorgeous fantail angels collapsing on the sand and the bright-colored neons and a velvet-and-white rasbora trying to leap out of the tank for oxygen. I ran off in the truck to get a chemical dissolving liquid from a tropical fish store but it was too late. Every last fish in the collection died. I am trying to write the experience in a short story, a symbol for people who choke other people with "good" actions that have bad consequences.

On a happy note the writing goes well and magazine editors continue to call and request pieces.

Back to Louisiana sans banjo on my knee.

Jenine and I took a wonderful voyage on a cruise boat down the Vermilion River north of Lafayette, Louisiana. We did not see alligators, but we saw lovely, lovely homes. We also took a great ride on the Mississippi River (salute to Captain Mark Twain!) aboard a ferry and we fell in love with Natchez, Mississippi, a must town for any lover of the South and Southern fiction and history. We caught a little sightseeing in the Mississippi Delta and Willie Morris country, then bopped homeward via the unspoiled Natchez Trace— sometimes as much a trail as highway. Jenine sends warm, warm wishes, and hi to Jim.

As ever,

Hank

1984 Jeannie Boyles telephoned Nuwer in Idaho to say her husband had died of a heart attack. Nuwer had disappointed and hurt Boyles in 1981, telling him he had to try moving from potboilers to serious work, and that number four would be the last book in the series. Three years later, Bob Gleason, the editor on the *Bounty Hunter* series, invited Nuwer for drinks with Gleason's wife at a New York restaurant. Gleason generously said his publisher was looking for new fiction ideas. Caught unprepared, Nuwer blurted that he was only looking to write " a quality book about hazing deaths." An angry, perhaps hurt Gleason told Nuwer he was throwing his career away and left without shaking hands. Gleason went on to publish many financially successful commercial books.

While Jenine Nuwer toiled as an editor in Idaho, Nuwer was on the road for a long list of magazines, including *Satellite Orbit, Outside, Saturday Evening Post, Inside Sports,* and a number of airline magazines. His fiction still sputtered, and he was at work at 4 a.m. most days to work on fiction and his serious writing, a habit he continued the rest of his life.

Henry Robert Nuwer died at home of a fatal stroke, while placing change into a jar to bring down-on-their-luck soldiers who wanted to call relatives long distance from a Buffalo Veteran's Hospital pay-phone. Jenine reached a South Carolina writer and fellow angler named Ron Rash who agreed to search for Nuwer on the Clemson campus. Nuwer was back at Clemson completing research for an article on football coach Danny Ford and player William Perry for *Inside Sports.*

Jenine flew in from Idaho to Buffalo for the funeral and Hank arrived from South Carolina. Nuwer's Buffalo State friend Joe Nikiel and Drew and Jim Brophy paid their respects at the funeral home, comforting Theresa Nuwer and the family.

39. Nuwer to Drew
Palacios, Texas
April 6, 1984

Dear Professor Bob:

I hope this finds you in good health. I'm sending greetings from Texas. It's taken a while to write because a lot has been going on in our lives. Unfortunately, we had a miscarriage and my dad had a stroke. I'm going to fly to Buffalo in May for the family's sake. If I take a taxi, perhaps you and I can get coffee.

I'm on assignment for *Outside Magazine* and *Inside Sports* in Texas. On Saturday I'll be back in South Carolina to do another assignment. I'm on the road now working for seven weeks. Jenine likes her editing job, but we are separated often. We live on a cattle ranch [in Idaho]—lots of Canada geese, red fox and coyotes. I had a request from an editor at Twayne to do a critical book on Hunter Thompson, but I had to turn it down with regret—no pay from them, no time from me.

We talk about you often and fondly.

Best,

Hank

40. Nuwer to Drew and Jim
Austin, Texas
April 29, 1984

Dear Professor Bob and Jim:

I'm still on my long, long business trip*, but I wanted to take a second to thank you both for the kind words at the wake. Jenine, my mother and I appreciated your visit and the lovely flowers for my dad.

I know our next visit or your next visit will be under pleasant conditions. I'll relish a visit from either of you.

Buffalo, somehow, seemed very different to me under the trying circumstances. I am reminded of T.S. Eliot's words:

And the end of all our exploring

Will be to arrive where we started

And know the place for the first time.

Jenine and my mother send their thanks and love to you both, as do I.

Hank

*Multiple stories for different magazines on University of Texas football and Coach Fred Akers.

41. Drew to Nuwer
Kenmore, New York
9 May 1984

Dear Hank and Jenine:

It is the restless time of year and my favorite month, one associated not only with the greening of the grass and trees and the springing of flowers but with getting ready for a flight to Ireland. I have been there in April and June, July and August, but May is the best month there, as it is here. May is cool in Ireland, and often wet, but it is tourist-free and especially beautiful. Ah, well, no Ireland this year! There is too much stuff in progress here and I am too creaky, but I intend to go again next year or some year. Meanwhile, it is beautiful here, even on the rainy days like today.

The notes from you both were gratefully received here. I have felt particularly close with you over recent weeks, and Jim regards you both as long-time friends. Jim is often slow to warm to people, the volatile Irish being but one-quarter of his strongly German background, but Hank's loyalty to me has long endeared him to Jim and Jenine is in high regard. We were both touched by the combination of warmth and quiet dignity in your mother, Hank, at such a difficult time. I hope that she is doing well. One day I think I shall give her a call just to say hello.

The long-delayed visit to Vermont was a good one. Jim, who still loves the state and used to go there frequently when my father was still living, had not crossed the border since 1975, and I had gone only once since 1975...a quick Easter weekend trip in 1981. Jim and I took a pleasant Adirondack route. The last leg of the drive was over Frost's Bread Loaf mountain past his memorial tablet and trail and then through Warren woods to Warren, the birth-place of my father, grandfather and great-grandfather (the lastly-named came, we think, from the Boston area where, we think, his father had come from County Kerry.)

A second cousin keeps the Pitcher Inn in the tiny town, which is very near ski places, and we had a little efficiency where we could get breakfast and take it out onto a balcony over the Mad River. All the brooks and rivers were full that week, and we saw many waterfalls on the hillsides. Before trees are leafed out, the mountain views are more revealing, though stark rather than lush.

We visited several relatives and significant sites. One day was Burlington and UVM, along with Randolph, with cemetery business and tsk-tsking over places vandalized by time and progress although perhaps over-romanticized by memory.

One local character just my age recognized me through the whiskers (and luckily I recognized her) in a local lunch-deli and screeched at me. "Jesus, he was cute guy," she announced to Jim and all by-sitters, "but look at *me* now, an old bag. Honey, how long are you going to be around? We used to live right across the street and play together. Jesus, we had fun!"

Actually, Enis didn't look too bad. Her daughter Elaine, a quarter century ago, was Miss Vermont and has given generous scholarship funds to the high school.

One day we spent in and near Woodstock, my mother's town and perhaps the most beautiful in the state, and tracked down one Fraser cousin on that side of the family. We checked out the townhouses and condos at Quechee Lakes nearby, a great place if one wanted to golf and clubhouse one's life away. One day we just loafed around the Warren area, picking up some baby larches to bring back for the yard and spending a half-hour in the largest stuffed animal store I had ever seen…bear-sized bears for $500, otters into which one could insert a hand and make head and paws do otter-things, and all presided over by a weird and enchanting mother and daughter team. I came away with a small red fox, being a fox-man as you know (along with wolves, bluejays). The dogs survived their kenneling and all is back to normal.

Some day I expect to go in to the college to hoe out another desk or file drawer and see a few people.

Jenine, I thank you for sending me *Satellite Orbit*. I like looking at your name on masthead, and I marvel at your editorial expertise in so technical a field, also at the good pieces in so technical a magazine, Hank's articles being especially good, of course. One of the retirement jobs, several of which I have actually accomplished, but few, on my list is an ordering of my Nuwer shelf to have in some kind of order the letters and the publications I have. I did get the Hemingways restored to order, but Jeffers and the Irish need a lot of work, along with Housman, Hank and Lord Byron.

Enough for us all, I hope that you are both fine and perhaps both by now in Hailey, though I forget Hank's calendar.

Love to you both,

Bob

PS I have to write an article on 1964 Shropshire visit for the *Housman Journal*, an annual in England of little fame. But it will be a pleasant task.

42. Nuwer to Drew
Cortez, Colorado
May 23, 1984

Dear Professor Bob and Jim:

On a hectic working trip. Colorado today, Grand Canyon tonight, Big Bend, Texas with Jenine meeting me next weekend on my assignment for *Outside* Magazine.

I recently went to the Hemingway monument and shrine in Sun Valley.

Love,

Hank

43. Nuwer to Drew
Hailey, Idaho
June 21, 1984

Dear Professor Bob:

Thanks for your last letter of 9 May. What wonderful details were in that one. Jenine and I loved bathing in your word pictures.

How goes the battle? Hope Jim is enjoying his summer off.

Jenine earned a promotion to senior editor. The company is expanding. There are rumblings about the publisher taking the operation to San Francisco or Boise or even back East.

Saturday Review went down the tubes and folded with my article on Stuart Gordon and David Mamet and the TV show E/R at press. What a sad ending for a revered magazine. I once had correspondence from Norman Cousins who edited the magazine in its heyday. I was paid for my article at least. Now a version of it will go into *Satellite Orbit*. Bruce Kinnaird, the editor, bought it, and I have to make revisions for the television market.

I know you're probably too busy to read the enclosed, but I revised my short story "Colic." Here also is another short story that was published in a college literary magazine. I wrote this one for fun.

I am also enclosing a little present, a letter signed by one of my favorite poets Thom Gunn (now that Philip Larkin's poetry has turned bitter). Thought you might like to have since Gunn is now a full-fledged "American" poet, though British-born, who told me he has no thoughts of going abroad to live.

I received a little bonus in the mail today. The University of Nebraska Press published an interview of mine in its new critical edition of *Shane.*

If you'd like to come to Hailey, give a holler. We'll drink to Ezra Pound, our native Idaho son, and lavish flowers on site of the Hemingway memorial overlooking the Wood River in Sun Valley nearby. Because it is almost certain the publisher will move the company, everyone is on hold and we're not buying additional furniture, but there are books on the shelves, wonderful roads to hike, and fine restaurants in Ketchum. We'd manage just fine.

Jenine and Christian send love to you and Jim, as do I. We talk about you two often.

Hank

Part III

Letters, Professor to Professor

(1985-1989)

44. Nuwer to Drew
Hailey, Idaho
February 18, 1985

Dear Professor Bob:

Greetings from out West. Our news is that the baby is due in six weeks. We are taking Lamaze classes. Son Chris will be here for Easter vacation when the baby is due.

Write when you have time. I'll be in Provo in a couple weeks to interview the champion Brigham Young footballers, and Jenine, though pregnant, will take the photographs. After the baby comes I'm headed to San Francisco to interview Coach Bill Walsh for three magazines.

Last December I bought a word processor for my writing.

Enough jabbering. Jenine sends love to you both, as do I.

Best, Hank

1985 Birth of Adam Robert Drew Nuwer, partially named after Fraser Drew.

The Nuwer family moved to Indiana so that Hank could accept a position at Ball State College in journalism.

Nuwer returned to Idaho's Wood River Valley on October 4 and 5 as co-director with historian Robert Waite of the Ezra Pound Centennial Conference held in Pound's hometown of Hailey. Among the guest speakers were Pound's longtime companion Olga Rudge and their daughter Mary de Rachewiltz, translator of her father's poetry and that of Robinson Jeffers and other American poets into Italian. Papers presented by Pound scholars were co-edited by Nuwer and Waite and published in a scholarly volume by Idaho State University Press.

45. Drew to Nuwer
Kenmore, New York
23 March 1985

Dear Hank and Jenine,

I am addressing this only to you two, since [son] Chris will not yet have arrived [to be a new godfather to his newborn brother] and since I do not plan to write to A.R.D. Nuwer until he is at least a year old and beginning to read and write. Even with such articulate and literate influences as his father, mother and names-source, he is not likely to start before one year.

You have been the chief source of thought and conversation here since night before last. I wonder if Hank was able to bring Jenine home today or if she and her son will be at St. Moritz [Sun Valley hospital] over the weekend. I rang the number a couple of times [yesterday] and got busy signals…I was a bit jittery about calling, anyhow, and lost my courage—I'm not sure why. Perhaps I think of you now, Jenine, as too fragile for jarring with a phone ring, or as too busy to take a call. Or maybe I was afraid of lapsing into sentimentality, though I did all right on the phone with you, Hank, in spite of excitement. Then I said [to Hank], "Well, anyhow, she must have our roses by now and know that we congratulate and love her," and then I probably phoned someone else and said again, "A baby is being named for me."

The postscripts came today, Hank. I'm glad to have the Howard Nemerov [letter he sent you]. He sounds like a nice guy for wanting [poet] John Morris included [in a magazine article Nuwer had done on Midwest writers].

Off to bed now easily. I'm tired but in good spirits. I hope that you are all doing fine. I hope, too, that you know how happy Hank's call made me Thursday night. Renewed congratulations to *everyone* there, and love to all.

Bob

46. Drew to the Nuwers
Kenmore, New York
1 April 1985

Dear Hank, Jenine, Chris, Adam,

It's a wild one here, the wind more March than April and every crocus shivering and wishing he were back in the bulb. I have my usual pain in the neck and shortness of breath and lethargy, but nothing new or worse—so complaints are minimal.

Your phone call Friday evening was very welcome. I usually dry up on the phone and dredge up banalities and old formulas, but I seem to remember burbling happily on at Jenine and, later, Hank. We were really glad to hear that all goes well.

No luck with airlines. United will not budge on extending my time at end or starting earlier, so that I have only the original 14 days in Casper [Wyoming].

So—all this, plus the realization that Adam will be only a bare (!) two months old in Late May and you still with hands full (there I go again!) as young parents, seems to indicate I'd better look to an Indiana or Buffalo or even a 1986 Idaho reunion—for an introduction. I come to this with reluctance but probably good sense, with my own anxieties the main stumbling block rather than anything else.

Jim and I hope the Beatrix Potter set will amuse you now, Hank, Jenine and Chris, and Adam somewhat later. I didn't grow up on Peter Rabbit and company, but I did visit Potter's old house in the English Lake Country in 1964, when Jim began collecting the Beswich (Royal Daulton) figurines of the animal characters. My Hartford friend, the late Bacon Collamore, had the world's best collection of Potter's botanical watercolors and drawings, as well as first editions of her books, and a couple weeks ago I complied with a request to do a brief memoir of Bac for the English *Beatrix Potter Newsletter*. So when I *do* get to visit you, I may be competing with Adam for use of bowl and whatever.

I hope the writing goes well, Hank. April 1985 will go down in history for you guys as Deadlines and Diapers.

I think I'll put on the Irish knit cap (well down over me ears) and other gear and get in at least a brief exercise walk. There's even a bit of sun.

Love to all,

Bob

47. Adam Nuwer to Drew, dictated at a precocious three weeks to his Daddy
Hailey, Idaho
April 11, 1985

Dear Professor Bob and Uncle Jim:

Hi. This is my first letter to you. Mom has given me some lessons in grammar and syntax. Bear with me until my vocabulary builds up, won't you?

What a wonderful surprise it was to get my present of a Beatrix Potter cup and bowl in this week's mail. My daddy and mommy also love it. To protect from chipping they say I can eat from them—when I am twenty-one. Dad says that poet Thom Gunn uses borrowed imagery from Beatrix Potter in his own work. I certainly hope Thom returns the imagery when he's through with it.

We still have snow on the ground. My mother Jenine bundles me to take me outside. Brother and daddy played catch with a baseball in the snow. The ball lasted three misses before it became too wet and heavy to throw.

My big brother Christian grabbed a nickel out of my hand last week that I found on the couch. I tried to put it in my mouth for safe storage, but big brother snatched it away. I don't know why mommy and daddy were upset with me. A guy shows a little enterprise to put away some money, and they come down on him. The nerve.

Brother and daddy went fishing on the Wood River four times last week. All they did mostly was drown bait and soak imitation flies. They caught only three fish in four trips, which isn't a bad batting average in baseball but pretty pitiful in a fishing contest. I'd have shown them a thing or two about catching trout had they shown the good sense to take me along.

You may have heard that I had a little problem in the hospital with my bilirubin test. I'm fine now, so I won't dwell on the past.

As you know, Daddy has applied for a teaching job in Indiana at Ball State University. I am practicing my Hoosier monotone. Daddy said to thank you for writing a reference.

Mommy's company *Satellite Orbit* magazine gave its editorial employees a 48-hour ultimatum yesterday to leave Hailey and commit to a Boise, Idaho move across the state or resign. She chose the last option. The company leaves Hailey June 10.

If Daddy screws up by drooling during his April 18-19 interview in Muncie, or if the Ball State dean insists that the journalism department hire a Ph.D. instead of a writer with experience, the Nuwer family will relocate to Indianapolis.

Daddy scored six months' worth of magazine assignments and asks you please not to worry about us. Contrary to myth, not all freelancers starve. I've offered to take a part-time job modeling. With my good looks how can I lose?

I can't wait to meet you, dear namesake and Uncle Jim. The way my mommy and daddy talk about you both, I know you must be special.

Guess I'll close. Daddy and mommy and brother Chris all have developed linguistic deficiencies. Instead of conducting a civil conversation with me, all they can do is say "goo goo" and make other obscene noises.

Love and thanks,

Little Adam Nuwer

48. Drew to Nuwer
Kenmore, New York
9 May 1985

Dear Hank,

This is another good day for walking down to the Kenmore post office, and I think I will stick something into the bag for Idaho. May has been very nice so far, and the backyard is full of tulips and primroses and other things. I suppose that my favorite little gold chain or laburnum will blossom just after I leave for Wyoming and lose its color just as I return. May seems to be the best time for being anywhere; I found it the best for Ireland after trying from the first of April to the first of September.

Tomorrow night is my dinner in honor of Jim's retirement. The guest-list stands at fifty-four, and all seems in readiness, including pianist, flowers, transportation for the wheel-less and ancient, super-cake, even our pastor from St. Louis Church to extend an ecumenical blessing (our Moslem friends cannot come, but we have Protestants, Catholics, Jews and question marks…it is the sort of thing which does not occur to me except for invocations and holidays).

As probably when I wrote to you last, I am still rereading *The Forsyte Saga* by John Galsworthy with pleasure and happily filling my time with small tasks of no great significance. I am feeling better, with some of the old energy back and the pains and aches no worse. I made my first visit to the college in many months, to smile benignly when the Fraser Drew Award for writing on an Irish subject, $100 from a fund collected by students during my last semester, was presented to a pleasant fellow for a sequence of poems; last year it went to a pretty girl for the symbolism of birds in Irish fiction. Two retiring professors were honored and much cheese and wine consumed.

Let me inquire about the new job, Hank!! I retain my interest from the viewpoint of your participation and want to know all about the job and place when we next meet. I do not expect detailed letters from you as you meet deadlines and cope with impending moves at end of summer and with family requirements. But of course I do want what detail you can spare about yourselves and particularly about a.r.d. and Chris. I wish I were going to see…the four of you.

Meanwhile, good luck with deadlines and diapers and love to all.

Bob

49. Drew to Nuwer
Casper, Wyoming
28 May 1985

Dear Hank, Jenine and Adam,

I feel quite frustrated at being only a state and the Continental Divide away from you and not seeing you, especially Adam. Let's hope we will make up for this soon.

The health report is surprisingly good. I got up to 10,000 feet in Rocky Mountain National Park and to 9600 in the Tetons without difficulty. I tire easily and was thrown into some anxiety by the United Airlines strike, but otherwise all seems to be OK. United cancelled the flight to Casper when I was between Chicago and Denver. My friends rescued me by driving to Denver. We had a fine long weekend in the Estes Park area and drove to Casper via Laramie, where I saw the University of Wyoming (I had a feeler from there in the late 1930s).

Last weekend we spent one night in Dubois and one in Jackson. I think the Grand Tetons are the most beautiful mountains I have ever seen. Roads were still uncrowded and we saw elk, moose, eagles, etc.

Jim and the dogs seem to be surviving at home, although Jim's great friend Mary Doe, 89, has just fallen and broken a hip and he is very busy. I expect to fly back Frontier-United on the 30th and am hoping for good connections. I will not be able to sprint like O.J. Simpson in his commercial through airports as I did in 1982 and 1983 when out here visiting.

I hope you are all great.

Love,

Bob

[PS] Best from Jim

50. Nuwer to Drew
Ball State University
June 30, 1985

Dear Professor Bob:

You deserve a long letter, but I'm afraid one will have to wait a couple weeks. Adam is thriving. Chris caught a giant lunker of a bass— approximately eight pounds. I'm finishing my collection of eight author interviews for an Idaho State University special issue of its periodical *Rendezvous*, prepare for my fall New Journalism graduate class, write four magazine features due in two weeks, deliver two lectures at Ball State's Midwest Writers Conference, and be a reasonably good dad and husband.

I am writing to see if I can coax you out of retirement. I am the co-director with Idaho State University Professor Bob Waite of the Ezra Pound Conference to be held in Hailey in October. I wonder if you would consider writing a paper titled "The Impact of Ezra Pound's Poetry." Your talk is intended for a general audience but can then be revised for Pound specialists in a book that will be published by Idaho State University Press. I'll deliver a paper titled "Pound As Editor." I personally will introduce you to the audience if you can attend.

We all send love. Best to you and Jim. We need to send him a retirement card. Adam is already eating crushed bananas and veggies. He laughs all the time. My mother is coming July 4 to see him in Indiana. She really seems to have perked up because of Adam. I'm glad you enjoyed Wyoming.

Love from all,

Hank

51. Drew to Nuwer
Kenmore, New York
5 July 1985

Dear Hank,

It was a sunny, bright Fourth here, but a bit warm for my northern taste. I recalled another sunny, bright Fourth, that of 1964, which Jim and I spent on the old steamer from Galway to the Aran Islands and back. It was a fine day but a great turning point in my life. I got a terrible sun-wind-salt burn, which turned to facial blisters that I carried through the Irish West and North and into Scotland. Until then I had been a sun worshipper in spite of my fair (not the best word) Irish skin. After then I never liked the hot sun again and have always sought the shade. It's more than the little skin cancers I have had. Something happened to the spirit as well as the skin that day.

One more Irish note, however. Jim and I will go to Niagara-on-the-Lake tomorrow to see George Bernard Shaw's *John Bull's Other Island*, his only really Irish play in spite of his Dublin birth. I saw it at the Abbey Theatre in 1969. We go to Niagara-on-the-Lake fairly often, liking the English character of the town and a restaurant-hotel called The Oban Inn after the Scottish hometown of the founders. We also go to Artpark at Lewiston on the U.S. side quite a bit for opera, ballet and the Preservation Hall Jazz Band of New Orleans, which comes every year and moves me greatly.

It was great to have Hank's letter today. I have not expected volumes from you. After all, you have a new job, a new baby, a new house, and all sorts of responsibilities. But it was great to hear. The news from a card from Jenine of Adam, also known as Adam Robert Drew, is great. Veggies and bananas and much laughter—he sounds just right. And Ernest the Fisherman would have approved of Chris' prowess. And here goes another quick bit of autobiography. I once made the White River Valley *Herald* for pulling an 14-inch rainbow trout from Chandler Brook near Randolph, a stream just about 11 inches wide. It was easily the high point of my not very distinguished sporting career.

Hank, I love you for asking me to speak at the Pound conference. But I couldn't. To begin with, I know Ezra Pound not at all well, which is shameful for a teacher of much modern poetry. Oh, I know his tremendous importance and something of his impact on T.S. Eliot and W.B. Yeats and I like some of the poems, too, but I would be an old fraud to write or speak about him, even to a general audience.

Also, I had to give up public appearances to speak or read papers quite a while back. Although I had enjoyed this sort of thing in the far past, it began to bother me. I would get advance stage fright and then get wet from head to toe with perspiration. But I am pleased to be asked and I am more pleased than you know, Hank, at your loyalty and confidence. I'll want to be in touch about the conference and your contributions to it in particular.

Don't worry about forgetting Jim's retirement. We started the celebration with a dinner on 10 May and he is still getting cards and notes.

Keep crunching those bananas, Adam.

Love,

Bob

52. Nuwer to Drew
Ball State University
August 14, 1985

Dear Professor Bob:

Hope this note finds you well and happy.

I'm headed for birthday number 39 in a week. Gad! I remember being a kid and wondering why Jack Benny chose to lie by claiming 39 as his age. I thought, why doesn't he pick a young age? Jenine and Chris chipped in for my requested present—a world atlas.

The bass are hitting nicely in our farm pond. Farmland is a pretty place to be, and it's nice and cool by the pond, a contrast to muggy Muncie. We've only flicked air conditioning on three times.

I'm attaching a short story of mine that will be in an airline magazine later this year. I finished my expanded *Rendezvousing with Contemporary Writers* book but haven't finished several magazine articles I must get done before my teaching duties begin. Actually, because I've been writing my lesson plans, I feel as if I have started teaching. In fact, in a couple hours I must don monkey suit and tie to speak at the Midwest Writers Conference. I'm nervous since two hundred people signed up. Hope no one boos.

Jenine has photographs this month in *Inside Sports* magazine to accompany my article.

Love,

Hank

53. Nuwer to Drew
Hailey, Idaho
October 6, 1985 (postcard of Hemingway's Wood River)

Dear Professor Bob:

The Ezra Pound conference was a success. I am charged with energy. On way back.

Warmest regards, Hank

54. Nuwer to Drew
Notre Dame University; South Bend, Indiana
November 25, 1985

Dear Professor Bob:

I loved your newsy addition to your last note. I'm afraid my note will be unpoetic. I just wanted to catch you up on our news.

This is my time off for Thanksgiving. Yesterday I was in Dallas to interview writer Kurt Vonnegut. I have read all of his books, and the interview went very well. Afterwards, he invited me to lunch. A good time was had by us both, I believe.

Today I'm writing predawn before my interview with Notre Dame's Digger Phelps. This is for two sports pieces for magazines.

Little ARD [Adam Robert Drew] has cut two bottom teeth. He's at the da-da, ba-ba stage of talking. He crawls like a wolf cub and seldom sleeps during the day.

I'll have dinner tonight with son Chris very late in Michigan. He had a good report card except for French and is doing well in soccer and wrestling.

I'm swamped with sixteen freelance articles and twelve "scholarly" author interviews since August. The Ezra Pound Conference in Idaho I co-chaired with Bob Waite a few weeks ago is history. I'm editing the proceedings in my spare time. I am glad I had a chance to walk amid the golden aspens of Sun Valley in October.

So the next big project is a labor of love. Bob and I plan to co-edit the proceedings of the Ezra Pound conference over Christmas break.

All goes well at Ball State other than the small pond, small school atmosphere. Novelist Jim Harrison calls your position as that of "town clown." Since August I've been asked to speak eight times. It's hard to convince people that time is ANY writer's most important resource. Yet one talk was to nearly one thousand junior high students and fun. They were a terrific audience and attentive. I also love my students and am very happy in the classroom. I am blessed with four good young writers. Our Ball State students have articles in *Seventeen* and *Writer's Digest* this month. My magazine students have interviews this month with TV personality Jane Pauley and Garfield creator Jim Davis for the magazine I advise.

I definitely am in love with teaching. Your own reputation has reached my classes. I have told them about your visits to Frost and Hemingway and how fortunate others and I were that you devoted your life to teaching. My memory of your classes is as clear as if I had attended the last one this morning.

November 22 passed. It was dad's birthday and my parents' anniversary before his death in 1984. The sadness about his passing hasn't diminished one bit. Does it ever?

Do you know that he only sent me one letter in his life? Writing was such a mysterious, painful task for him. My mother misses him terribly. She had such a nice visit with us in Farmland last summer.

Time to check all notes before the interview with Digger Phelps.

Oh, Buffalo State was rated very highly in *U.S. News & World Report* this week!

Love,

Hank

1986 The *New York Times* reported the death of former Provincetown Players actress Norma Millay Ellis, sister of poet Edna St. Vincent Millay and guardian of her late sister's literary estate. Drew had corresponded with Ellis and twice visited her at her Steepletop (named for a wildflower on the property) farm in Austerlitz, New York, the residence of Millay until her death in 1950. Drew had long been a Millay admirer and collector. During one visit at Ellis's pool, she rescued a wood mouse that had fallen into the water. She generously gave the professor a page of an Edna Millay worksheet, the typescript corrected in the poet's own hand of one of the three "sonnets in tetrameter" from "Huntsman, What Quarry?"

Nuwer's friend David Harrison, despondent over his inability to sell screenplays or creative work of importance, ended his life by gunshot on December 27 on a beach in Venice, California. Months earlier Nuwer had stayed with Harrison at his apartment on a New York working trip, but had taken time to see a Sam Shepard play with Harrison at the Promenade Theater.

55. Nuwer to Drew
Ball State University
January 4, 1986

Dear Professor Bob:

Happy New Year! I wonder if I can call on you for a reference? As the enclosed brochure indicates, NASA has an opening for one person to be chosen journalist-in-space. The university will grant me a leave if I am selected. To do this I've lost about eighteen pounds in a month and have twelve to go. I've joined the YMCA, sworn off sweets, meats, all alcohol, all snacks.

The idea is that the successful applicant must be a trained communicator who can bring a new perspective to live reports and mission history. They want someone with poise in front of a TV camera. I plan to cite my experience with the Tom Snyder *Tomorrow Show, PM Magazine* and etcetera. The applicant must have the ability to let the rest of the world share his or her experience.*

Love from all of us,

Hank

* Ed. Walter Cronkite was a finalist and probably would have gone into space had not the Reagan administration insisted on sending a teacher first. The program never happened because of the tragic Challenger explosion, killing crew and teacher Christine McAuliffe.

56. Drew to Nuwer
Kenmore, New York
7 January, 1986

Hank,

RE: Journalist-in-Space Project.

I want to get reference into mail this afternoon.

I think this is a great idea and you are the ideal person to do it.

Love to all, Bob

57. Nuwer to Drew and Jim Brophy
Farmland, Indiana
March 14, 1986

Dear Professor Bob and Jim:

This is a note to thank you for Adam's bank—it has to be the fanciest kid bank outside of a Rockefeller baby's bedroom. It gleams on the shelf alongside the Beatrix Potter present you gave him at birth.

Thank you for your A.E. Housman essay. "The chisel-marks never show"—I love that phrase.

We had a rainstorm here that made all our snow vanish in an afternoon. When I peeked out the window after a writing session I saw that only the loins of a snowman remained.

Next, our sad news, and it is very sad. Shane Howard, Jenine's brother, a student at Indiana University-Purdue University, Indianapolis (IUPUI) passed away with viral meningitis two weeks back.

We have already grieved. Now comes the long, slow part of sorrow as James Dickey calls the process.

Adam was a joy to have around as the family came in from North Carolina to assist Shane's widow Martina, a sweet young woman from Switzerland. Shane was a good student, a fine athlete, and a terribly nice man. I wish I had his disposition.

Adam now waves goodbye, extends his arms to "How big is Adam?" questions, knows his eyes, ears, mouth and nose. He routinely starts games of peekaboo, flirts shamefully with waitresses and my students. He has attended three college classes of mine as I watch him while Jenine lectures on copy editing. He loves to hear stories told and read.

Things are hectic. The one bad thing about being a writer on campus, as happened in Clemson, is that he or she must deal with dozens of requests from nice, well-meaning people to speak, judge this contest, visit this class, drop by this event, go to lunch with the visiting writer or editor.

"You'll have so much in common. You both write."

Unspoken rejoinder: "Yes, Harold Robbins and John Updike would make a merry pair at the 21 Club, wouldn't they?"

Maybe it is different at a major university where writers are abundant, sharing oxygen in the same big pond.

At a smaller school, to mix imagery beyond repair, a writer is a combination draft horse and race horse. You must pull your share, attend every committee meeting, take on all service responsibilities that the rest do, and then after you're sufficiently lathered, show up at the county fair, too, to race the next town over's fastest horse so that your folks can bet on you.

Why am I telling someone all this who has a telephone access code?

I'd better stop complaining. I should tell you that the snow has melted here in Indiana. The ground smells sweet and pungent, by turns and depending where you walk. The ice is gone from our farm pond, and I've already dropped a line in pursuit of bass.

Chris comes here for ten days at the end of the month. He made the volleyball team and had a short story submitted by his English teacher to a national contest.

The interview with George Plimpton I did in New York was great fun. Old friend David Harrison and I saw Sam Shepard's *A Lie of the Mind*—scary and wonderful and wise—off-Broadway.

My book-length collection of interviews for Idaho State University Press is overdue from the printers, and I'm anxious over it.

My magazine sequence at Ball State has placed more students in internships at *Writer's Digest, Kiwanis* magazine and *Outdoor Indiana* this year. I have a couple of fine students and I love one of my writing classes especially.

Happy St. Patrick's Day, b'gorra.

Love,

Hank

58. Drew to Hank Nuwer
Kenmore, New York
25 April 1986

Dear Hank:

Two days ago arrived *Rendezvous* [a special issue of the Idaho State University humanities magazine with eight interviews by Nuwer conducted with contemporary writers]. I do not need to tell you that I like the dedication. I accept Ron Rash [Nuwer's old Clemson fishing companion and a poet and novelist] and Randy Figurski [former student who taught Nuwer to use a computer] on faith and cannot think of better dedicatees than the other persons. For my inclusion, many thanks and more appreciation than I can easily express to you.

The interviews are great. Frankly I had expected that they would be, but I wondered how many I could read before becoming aware and perhaps tired of the format, the interview. No weariness at all, perhaps because you handle the interview situation so easily, comfortably. The reader forgets that this is question-and-answer as it becomes conversation, an informal kind of essay or narrative or whatever. Perhaps, too, your wise choice of interview subjects who are so various and different.

My own experience with the eight was also quite varied. I had read quite a bit of Thom Gunn, had heard a lot about Maurice Sendak from my collector friend, now dead, Bacon Collamore. James Dickey's name had crossed my vision frequently, and I knew a little of Jim Harrison, I think, from you. David Mamet, Mark Steadman, Harry Crews and William Least Heat Moon were completely new to me. This very variety was great fun.

You both inform and entertain. I feel that I know quite a lot about these guys, and you certainly made them interesting, often downright vivid. Your preliminary material before each interview is not only helpful but also varied and good reading. There seems to me to be nothing routine or repetitive or awkward anywhere. One comes away with the feeling that you liked what you were doing. I liked editor Bob Waite's introduction. As Waite comments, [you have] "not a bad life at all."

What you have done and you say to Waite give me much justification for much of the teaching I did. You are interested in the story behind the stories, the soul behind the words. My colleagues used to berate me for not teaching the art product for itself alone with no consideration of the artist. To me this would have been a sterile and soulless procedure. I think my classes would have been smaller and quieter, traffic into my office lighter, correspondence after retirement less.

Will phone your mother one day.

Love to you all and thanks,

Bob

59. Drew to Nuwer
Kenmore, New York
26 May 1986

Dear Hank and Jenine,

I have just read Hemingway's *The Garden of Eden*. As for Ernest's book, it was a severely edited unfinished and often-laid-aside manuscript. The result is not up to his best books. But it has one fine story within the story, and it is an interesting example of how a writer makes up people and events out of people and events he knew. Knowing his life, I can see where this book came from, but it is not autobiography. I shall read it again more carefully. Right now I find it less attractive than his best books and the story line a little thin. In places, too, it almost seems like self-parody, a fault of the 1950 book, *Across the River and Into the Trees*. It is surely made from one of the great piles of unpublished manuscript, which I saw in the steamer trunk at Mary's apartment the Thanksgiving after Ernest shot himself, along with the piles that turned into *A Moveable Feast, Islands in the Stream*, and *The Dangerous Summer*.

I was delighted some time ago to receive the copy of the student publication Hank advises at Ball State. The publication is surely well above the level of most student publications that I have seen, attesting, I am sure, to good instruction and mentorship and, perhaps, also to superior native ability. Congratulations, Hank.

James (Jim) Brasch, who is Professor of English at McMaster University in Ontario, a Steinbeck and Hemingway man, checked in by mail last week as he does every decade or so. He was in a fine class I had back in the early 1950s with his wife Dolores Mertz, Heidi Lyon Mahoney, Tom Ingraham (who wrote to Hemingway and got a reply which his daughter brought to my class 25 years later—Tom died young), and a couple of other memorable students. Jim and I were never close but respected one another's "scholarly" instincts.

I wish you a great summer for writing, Hank.

Love to you all,

Bob

60. Drew to Nuwer
Kenmore, New York
11 October 1986

Dear Jenine, Hank, and Adam,

When Jim, the dogs, and I returned from three days in Westfield yesterday afternoon, we found among the bills and junk mail a great letter from Indiana and pictures. As for the pictures the one of ardn [Adam Robert Drew Nuwer] and Former Professor Bob Drew in which the latter has a full grin or laugh is, we think, a masterpiece.

I tend to hate any picture of me because I look my chronological age or older, but this one really pleases me, especially the contrast between the gravity of Adam and the jollity of me. In the others, he looks even more solemn and I even more old. There is, however, the tenderness and humor of my holding him as if he were extremely fragile china, which he ain't. I like the Broadway Market picture of the three male Nuwers (Hank, Chris, Adam), and I am glad to have them all. Thank you.

I am glad that you took a bit of time to wander in Polonia when you were here. Buffalo is one of the great Polish cities, and it is good for Hank and his boys to stay in touch with that side of their heritage. National backgrounds fascinate me, and especially when they are mixed or have wild juxtapositions. Hank is German and Polish; Jim is German and Irish—75 percent German, 25 percent Irish. My mix is so strained through several generations of Vermont that it is hard to tell the percentages, but it isn't far from 25 percent Scots, 25 percent English, 50 percent Irish. I am sure of the Scots, and the English and Irish could be closer to 37.5 percent each.

As a little boy I grew up fanatically pro-French, being a World War I kid born in 1913. I learned to read from the comics and the newspaper accounts of the war, and I still have relics of that Francophile attitude even though I have never been on the Continent.

Now it is Sunday, 12 October, my parents' wedding anniversary from 1909! My mother would be 97, my father 106 (like I felt when I awoke this morning).

For now, love to you all from here.

Bob.

1987 Drew and Brophy become canoeing enthusiasts in their red canoe. Neighbors dubbed the two Lewis and Clark.

61. Drew to Nuwer
Kenmore, New York
5 January 1987

Please seat yourselves firmly before reading further, Adam on Jenine, Jenine on Hank. If you wish, for you will need a steady and firm foundation. About ten days ago we arrived at a decision and within four days had sold this house and bought another. I would have bet a considerable sum on my staying here in this house until the time for going underground by my parents in Randolph, Vermont, for we had this place just about as we wanted it after ten years.

One day, however, Jim saw a place on the Niagara escarpment in woods and came home to tell me about it. I scoffed and sent up minatory puffs of smoke and rumbled but agreed to ride up to see it. One look and I was hooked, too, and I have been alternately dismayed and excited ever since. This place sold before its description hit the realtors' sheets, the buyers being a U.S. Congressman and family.

This change of direction, or whatever, seems to have enlivened me somewhat, when I am not worrying about the physical move...We have 103 liquor boxes all packed (but not with liquor)...I have not yet started on books, however. Yike!

Love,

Bob

1988 Nuwer presented paper titled "Tom Wolfe Among the New Journalists" at Randolph-Macon College in Virginia at a Tom Wolfe Symposium on September 15-16 with Wolfe himself delivering main address.

Nuwer received a Poynter Institute award for journalism teaching.

Nuwer was nominated by Ball State University for a C.A.S.E. national outstanding professor of the year award. He was named Outstanding Adviser of the Year by Ball State students.

62. Nuwer to Drew
Muncie, Indiana
April 6, 1988

Dear Professor Bob:

Jenine and I appreciated your wonderful John Masefield gifts of letter and signed photograph you sent Adam. Knowing this is the last Masefield letter in your possession makes it a particularly special present. We will treasure it and your accompanying letter to Adam until he is old enough to appreciate its significance and can write you a proper letter himself. You see, this obligates you to hang around on this planet until your mid-nineties, at the least.

Flu season has struck. I've been in the week for days. Last month I had a good trip to New York City where I delivered three lectures in two days for College Media Advisers. One on fiction techniques in nonfiction was jammed with listeners. I also was in Arkansas fishing on assignment with Jerry McKinnis, host of *The Fishin' Hole* on cable.

We will be in Buffalo on August 20. Can we reserve August 21 for lunch?

Love,

Hank

63. Drew to Nuwer
Lockport, New York
16 April 1988

Dear Hank:

It pleases me that you liked the John Masefield book, Masefield signature and letter for Adam. Let's hope it doesn't in some supernatural way predispose him toward a career under sail or beating out the time for sonnets.

21 August is noted on calendar for lunch. Now we'll try not to schedule a visit to Vermont for that time. It will be good to see you.

The violets and trilliums are up in the woods here, and tulips and daffodils along the drive and on the lawn. Buds bud, and it should be a beautiful spring. The recent spaification of my bathtub seems to be helping the arthritis; the dogs stand outside the door, suspicious of the gurgling of the jets. On most days I walk quite well.

Love, Bob

PS My long-time friend (BSC '48) Bea Beckman died of cancer in Chicago two weeks ago. I remember many good things such as: When she was about to get her M.A. at Canisius in 1952, and I was about to get my Ph.D. at the University of Buffalo, I was getting ready for one of the final [written examinations] on a minor in the mediaeval period and one of my eyes swelled and closed. I called Bea, who appeared in a half-hour with shopping bag full, bathed my eye, sent me to bed, cooked dinner, did the dishes, and read Chaucer and Malory to me for several hours. Her thesis was on Stephen Vincent Benet, and last week came a large box with Bea's collection of SVB first editions. [and] also an antique pewter hurricane lamp for Jim. Bea had come here for a day last fall. We had a great reunion but all knew it was the last one. She was 63, a fine editor with an unerring ear and eye for our language and a beautiful voice for singing and speech.

64. Drew to Nuwer
Lockport, New York
31 May 1988

Dear Jenine, Hank and Adam,

First of all, thank you for the great pictures. The big one [Adam's nursery school photo] has been slipped in front of a picture of myself sitting at a window of Yeats's tower in County Galway and has been moved to the Jeffers section. The smaller one with [Adam and his dog] Dusty is on my desk right now and could end up in my wallet along with the early picture [of Adam] with me on Danbury Lane, or in the Nuwer pages of my Album of Family and Friends (1913 -). It is a happy picture of two friends. As in all the pictures, what a great-looking boy!

Much news in your letter! I was delighted by the outstanding adviser award, all-university, and by the nomination for the CASE Award. I cannot feign wide-eyed, hush-voiced surprise at these, but isn't it wonderful to see someone honored who has really put his head and his heart and his hands all into his work?

Chris appears to be a versatile athlete: even within the area of track and field, that is quite a range from the (to me) unglamorous shotput to the soaring pole vault and the exciting relay. I was never good at anything, being undersized, book-oriented and klutzy, but I have been a great spectator for decades, especially at football, basketball, track and tennis. Like his father, Chris seems to be a natural.

Jim and I were interested to hear of the gardening side of you, Jenine, and also [of] Adam. Jim could work outside happily from eight to eight all summer. Even days when I was agile and supple, I didn't have his enthusiasm, but I like being outside up in the country here.

Right now our rhododendrons are at their height. We have eighteen, the largest of which were here when we bought the place. Most are of the familiar orchid shade, but we have one that is dark red and three white ones. Also at their height of bloom just now are our two small laburnums (about 6 feet high), which were the first acquisitions here. Both are laden with the chains of yellow bloom, which give them their other name of gold-chain tree. A couple of weeks ago we planted 576 orange-red impatiens plants which will stay around into mid-fall and keep adding to their size and color.

We are both OK. Jim has worked off some weight and looks good. My pot increaseth and I shall complete my third quarter of a century in June. I probably bemoaned that in the last letter, too!

It has been a beautiful spring, and I hate to see an end of May. So, of course, did A.E. Housman, who made better music of his complaint than I do: "May will be fine next year as like as not – Oh, aye, but then I shall be twenty-four." On that fine note I sign off with love to you all.

Bob

65. Drew to Nuwer
Lockport, New York
19 September 1988

Dear Hank, Jenine and Adam (and Chris, should he have hopped a pre-Easter bunny down from Ann Arbor):

The card with Hemingway the Fisherman reached us here shortly after the final move. I was happy to hear of the Poynter Institute award.

Love to you all,

Bob

1989 Nuwer's former associate H.B. (Toby) Halicki (1940-1989) died in Western New York on August 20, while filming the sequel to *Gone in 60 Seconds*. A cable snapped, causing a chain reaction that ended in a telephone pole snapping and striking him.

The Nuwer family rented out their Muncie house and moved to a house and 24 acres in Stanford, Indiana, outside Bloomington as Nuwer finished *Broken Pledges*.

66. Nuwer to Drew
Muncie, Indiana
May 1, 1989

Dear Professor Bob:

It's a cold May 1 here in Muncie, but I have a warm feeling thinking of you and Jim sitting in front of a warm Buffalo fire with ye dogs curled at your feet.

I'm going to attempt once again to write without teaching. I didn't know if I should get a one-year absence from Ball State to finish *Broken Pledges*, *Steroids*, and my novel, or simply quit. Since I have no intention of returning to Ball State if my books do well, I solved the ethical dilemma by handing in my own pink slip. Some other writer may be able to work twenty hours a week at a teaching job, but it takes me forty to sixty hours a week to do all that I know needs doing.

Forcing this decision was the fact that my co-writer on the novel, Jim Noble, has suffered a heart attack, leaving him with a small percentage of healthy heart. He had ignored the pain for two days before letting his wife take him to the hospital. This gives us urgency to finish our project. I don't know that I told you much about Jim. He's been a logger, a country singer, a law enforcement officer, a sixth-grade dropout. He's a fine storyteller and a funny, funny man.

In addition, I'm the staff writer for *Fireside Companion*. All these assignments and teaching were in addition to weekly faculty meetings, committee assignments, mostly unpaid speaking engagements and awards banquet responsibilities. Tonight I write a speech for a Wednesday talk to the Kiwanis Club.

I'll close. Here is a tape of a recent TV appearance. I thought you might like seeing it.

Love,

Hank

67. Nuwer to Drew
Muncie, Indiana
June 5, 1989

Dear Professor Bob:

I wanted to send you a copy of the attached article on "Mentors" written for *Men's Fitness* magazine. Hope you like your brief mention, which is heartfelt.

Also, I want to share some news, albeit unpleasant. In no particular order our house was struck by lightning, destroying computer, furnace, modem, tape recorder, and appliances; our cat Dixie was killed by a driver on our quiet street; a thief stole Chris's gold chain with his football number on it that I had bought him, and our Ford's exterior was destroyed in a hailstorm.

The writing for my *Broken Pledges* and *Steroids* books goes well. If you can find the current issue of *Sport* magazine I have an essay in it.

I just was in Minnesota to interview a plant specialist near ninety who has taken up the cause of trying to bring back the American chestnut, an important wood and nut tree destroyed by blight, and am writing an essay on him for *Fireside Companion*.

My ex Alice said she saw you quoted in some celebrity biography, (maybe Tyrone Power or Gary Cooper?) in regard to your visit in Cuba with Hemingway. Alice says hello to you.

Just talked to Jenine on the phone. She conveys her love, as do I.

Hank

68. Nuwer to Drew
Bloomington, Indiana
September 16, 1989

Dear Professor Bob:

Yay! We are pleased and relieved by your encouraging medical report. So glad that all goes well with important Drew plumbing fixtures. Hope you can handle rising blood pressure without drugs. Drugs really played havoc with my Dad's health. Do keep us informed.

Adam loves Bloomington, and he dances on the streets. He's such a joyous kid. He and Chris are listed in the index of my new book on athletic recruiting for Franklin Watts. It was fun to show Adam his name.

Here is my book *Recruiting in Sports* to clutter your book shelves.

I'll write later.

Love,

Hank

69. Nuwer to Drew
Bloomington, Indiana
October 1, 1989

The leaves on these 24 acres outside Bloomington we rent in Stanford are magnificent. Down the road is a red-leafed oak tree that would break your heart with joy and send you back in time to Vermont.

Adam is at my favorite former student's house visiting her, and Jenine is in Chicago on a freelance magazine assignment. I've been up two days and two nights writing (see result attached) and loving it. My God, to be free to write any time I want! Is that heaven or what?

Time to put on another pot of coffee. It's a lovely night in Indiana. You can get a great eye-load of stars in the middle of the night, and the Big Dipper is clearly stamped on the sky. Here is a constant, rippling Indiana wind that refreshes, totally the opposite of those hot, uncomfortable Santa Ana winds that beset Southern California in the winter.

Here are two copies of Jenine's freelance magazine *Fireside Companion*. You might like reading the story "Season for a Son" that my former Midwest Writers conference student Gary Eller wrote. He has graduated already from the Iowa Writers program with his MFA. He lives in Ames writing fiction full-time while his wife supports them as a librarian. I'm hopeful he has a big novel in him but try to encourage, not coerce.

I'm drooling over those Jeffers books you mentioned buying last letter. Back in 1976 I gave a paper at the Robinson Jeffers Conference in Ashland, Oregon, and so did Tim Hunt, who was then a Ph.D. candidate at the University of Utah. I remember Hunt as bright, ambitious, eager to finish his doctoral work, and a comer. My interlocutor was Frederick I. Carpenter who talked about being a Vietnam War protestor. He gave me tough but fair questions following the reading of my paper. His first question was to compare the pessimistic outlook of Walter Van Tilburg Clark, Jeffers and Eugene O'Neill.

Also at that conference was Brother Antonius [William Everson, a Jeffers scholar], hairy as a goat, slow-talking, very sweet, with good insights into Jeffers and not a bad poet himself. Robert Brophy [editor of the *Robinson Jeffers Newsletter*] was there, nice man, and the father of adopted babies from Asia.

I am putting in a second copy of *Fireside Companion* with my Elbert Hubbard essay for the next time you see Sister Joseph in the Butler Library Special Collections. She helped me with my research on

Hubbard, and a second article of mine will appear in the *Gale Dictionary of Literary Biography* soon. I also just finished an essay on the *Overland Monthly* for another scholarly book to keep my pen dipped in the blood of the academic world.

Best to Jim.

Love, Hank

70. Drew to Nuwer
Lockport, New York
19 November 1989

To Hank,

This key is a keepsake to you from my undergraduate days at the University of Vermont. Our college newspaper was called *The Vermont Cynic*. I was a reporter as a freshman, news editor as a sophomore and was elected by the whole board, editor in chief for the year, which included second semester junior and first semester senior. I think this was the most satisfying activity of my University of Vermont years, which were a good blend of the academic and social.

This key I used to wear on a watch fob with my Phi Beta Kappa key. I can't think of any practical use you could make of it, but you seemed the appropriate recipient.

Love, Bob

Part IV

Letters, Friend to Friend

(1990-1998)

71. Drew to Nuwer
Lockport, New York
15 January 1990

Dear Jenine and Boys-of-all ages,

There hasn't been much to write about and so I haven't written since before the holidays. The situation hasn't changed but I feel an inclination to send Hank an unobtrusive pat on the back for his long hard hours of work. Once deadline has been met, you all deserve at least a brief respite from the working schedule.

I've been browsing in the Vonnegut book of interviews with your fine one, which came at Christmas (Thanks!), and I confess that now and then I sneak back into the *Men's Fitness* issue when I need reassurance that those decades of college teaching were something more than a relatively simple way of managing a decent living.

I still think that I lived at the right time for me. I do not, like E.A. Robinson's Miniver Cheevy, "miss the medieval grace of iron clothing," and certainly I do not wish that I were graduating from the University of Vermont or Duke University in June of 1990.

Ancient Greece in the time of Pericles? No.

Certainly not Colonial North America.

How about you? England before 1914, or South Pacific before missionaries, or the big chance of late-middle Twenty-First Century?

Occasionally the routine breaks pleasantly. For instance, yesterday we went to Amherst for brunch at home of Steve and Fran Sherwin. A delightful four-hour session for which I was willing to sacrifice the Denver-Cleveland football game.

The Sherwins had, as promised, in addition to the traditional & unnecessary sausages and eggs and coffee cake, a magnificent home prepared white fish salad and my favorite lox, cream cheese, red onion and toasted bagels. Plus abundant coffee and a beautiful bowl of fresh fruit in all colors to which rum had been added. Great!

Fran Sherwin has always been my favorite faculty wife, and Steve my ally since he came to the college a decade after me. Their older son flew in from New Orleans in time to take over what brunch we had left untouched. He is a bassoonist in a New Orleans symphony, and he and wife & three-year-old son have just moved to N.O. from Denver. Jonathan has an audition in Toronto this week. The younger Sherwin son is a doctor in Chicago. Interesting family. Steve retired from BSC last year, Fran will work a little longer at the University of Buffalo.

Jim and I hope that all three of you have a fine 1990.

Love, Bob

1990 Nuwer's book *Broken Pledges: The Deadly Rite of Hazing* was released in October and led to an appearance on the *Joan Rivers Show* with Eileen Stevens, mother of Chuck Stenzel , the hazing victim who died at Alfred University in 1978.

Last-minute travel for research created a huge balloon debt on his credit card and made it necessary for him to scramble for full-time work and more magazine freelancing. He sent a single application for a job off to Rodale Press and was hired to work at its sprawling offices in Pennsylvania on books for its *Prevention* [magazine] imprint.

72. Drew to Nuwer
Lockport, New York
3 August 1990

Dear Hank,

I hope that you will be able to get to Buffalo for the Labor Day weekend. We are likely to be here and it would be fine to hear your voice and finer to see you. I know, however, how difficult it is to find a spare hour in a brief weekend with family reunions.

The Rodale work sounds tolerable, if not ideal, and if it leaves night hours for better work, that is good. I am sorry that you had to leave the Bloomington, Indiana area, but perhaps one day you can go back.

Last night Jim and I went to an outdoor carillon concert in Williamsville and enjoyed two diversions with the music: a pair of cardinals and a young boy with his first two-wheeler. I imagined him as Adam. It was pleasant strolling around Jim's childhood streets in Williamsville after an early car parking. I encountered an old-time student of the '57 vintage whose wife claimed that I had routed their honeymoon to include Frost's Ripton, Edna St. Vincent Millay's Austerlitz hideaway at Steepletop, and other east-of-the Hudson literary locales.

I have been reading the one unread Hemingway, *The Dangerous Summer*, and a new *Hemingway in Spain* by Edward E. Stanton, which begins suspiciously with a paragraph quoted from a 1951 letter from Hemingway to me. It was fun to see that.

No writing but much reading, including one a month or so ago about Vienna in 1913, when weirdly enough Hitler, Stalin, Freud, Jung and Trotsky were all living there!

Not in the same lodging.

Love to all. There will be better days.

Bob

73. Drew to Nuwer
Lockport, New York
25 October, 1990

Dear Hank,

Today my great friend, Louise Townsend Nicholl, would have been 95. Several Latin quotations, which I'll spare you, throng the mind on the passage of time. Outside the windows, leaves at their peak of red and gold fall slowly to illustrate the mood.

Yesterday the handsome book *Broken Pledges* came. The jacket with its arresting colors, title, subtitle, author's name and photograph, and good blurb should attract readers. I hope there will be good reviews in good places.

The dedication to me surprises and moves deeply. Thank you very much. Any "debt" you feel to the long-ago teacher has been lovingly paid, and more than adequately. But I am deeply pleased and honored, and highly appreciative of the company I keep [in the dedication].

I have read excellent preface, looked at well-chosen photographs, and scanned appendix. I'll not say that I'll enjoy reading the book on hazing deaths—it will be hard to read in one sense—but I'll read it with tremendous interest, and I'm glad you tackled this difficult assignment. The book had to be done, and you did it.

I'll write again with the usual barrage of trivia, but for now I wanted to acknowledge at once the arrival of *Broken Pledges*.

Congratulations, and love to all Nuwers.

Bob

1991 The business manager of Hall of Fame baseball pitcher Ferguson Jenkins wanted to see if Jenkins and Hank were compatible to write the athlete's life story. Nuwer traveled to New York and met Jenkins in a hotel suite. During constant interruptions by Jenkins's girlfriend who was high strung and intense, Nuwer played with the player's stepson Raymond and read to his young daughter. Finally, bored, she pressured Jenkins to leave the meeting to go shopping. Unable to see himself cooped up for two or three months at Jenkins's house with the nervous and flighty girlfriend around, and upset that Jenkins omitted telling him he already had three books published, Nuwer declined the offer to move to the pitcher's Oklahoma ranch to co-write the book. In January 1993, the girlfriend Cynthia Takieddine killed Fergie's daughter Samantha and took her own life by carbon monoxide poisoning in the athlete's Bronco on his Oklahoma ranch.

Financially, Rodale's decent salary allowed Nuwer to climb at least part of the way out of a financial hole he'd put himself and his family in with research trips for *Broken Pledges*. He contributed chapters to four published Rodale books on health in a little over a year. He kept his hand in teaching by offering a continuing studies class in health and science writing for Temple University, Ambler.

74. Drew to Nuwer
Lockport, New York
25 February, 1991

Dear Hank,

I hope you are all well. Jim is OK. He has been going to New York City to buy a small apartment for renting. Eventually, when bereaved of all Buffalo-area connections, he'd like to live in New York City. Not I.

I lost a good former student last month—Richard Lautz, BSC '56, Arkansas M.A., University of Pennsylvania Ph.D., Professor of English at LaSalle University. He was only 55—kidney abscesses, septicemia, etc. Very sad—a productive, civilized guy. *

Also another student, 61, an ex-model, one of the brightest and most beautiful ladies, Aileen Leatherbarrow Buckley, last month. It is unnatural to survive one's children or students.

Stay safe, well.

Love,

Bob

* Ed. Professor Lautz was an excellent poetry editor (Four Quarters magazine), distinguished teacher and book collector of first-edition poetry, who was inspired as an undergraduate by Fraser Drew. The Lautz Special Collection at LaSalle contains his vast collection, including numerous signed volumes].

75. Drew to Nuwer
Lockport, New York
30 July 1991

Dear Jenine and Nuwermen,

The summer has gone well except that my old bones are horizontal more than I'd choose—little energy. However, I'm planning on a Vermont expedition.

Another not-quite-surprise, the arrival of Brigid Murray's first novel, *Figures in a Landscape*, Chapman, London, inscribed "For Bob who first encouraged me to write and whose belief helped me to survive, with gratitude and love, Brigid."

The writer, who used to call herself "Sheila" Murray, is the young potter turned watercolorist who had the craft center at Dunquin, County Kerry. She used to time her deliveries to various Irish shops for my visits in '69, '70, '71 and '72, and would drive me along over mountain passes and along seaside fields I wouldn't otherwise have seen. I handled lodging, petrol and food. She used to read me poetry and prose written in spare hours. Later she had success with her watercolors and one-woman shows in Berlin, Paris and English cities. I have a couple of watercolors here as well as a wall-hanging and some little cups and a silk scarf from her earlier years. This book is impressive although the story is grim, the north Yorkshire setting (where she now lives) stark, the detail often grimy and smelly, the people hardly huggable.

Sheila Murray was the daughter of Irish parents living in the north of Yorkshire in England and returned there herself after a decade in the far southwest of Ireland on a hillside looking across the Blasket Sound at the offshore Blasket Islands. When I met her she was a craftswoman at pottery, silk scarves and wall hangings, but she was a good poet and a good cook. Sheila packed great lunches. If we ate at the craft shop, she and partner Jean Yetts cooked great meals. Sheila rode me over some great coastal roads and mountain passes I would not have seen otherwise. I have some great letters from her but none recently. She had changed her name from Sheila to Brigid after discovering that she had been preceded by a Sheila who had died at birth. "I wanted a name of my own," she said, "instead of sharing with a dead sister."

It was good to hear your voice on the phone, Hank. I hope the plans for the Ferguson Jenkins book develop well.

Love,

Bob

76. Nuwer to Drew
Fogelsville, Pennsylvania
August 12, 1991

Dear Professor Bob:

I fondly remember letters in which you spoke of visits to Ireland that were made better by Brigid Murray's guided tours. I'm so pleased that she has a novel out. In this lifetime I plan to read it, maybe next year if I can steal some time.

I've read 15 books since leaving Rodale in mid-June, but my resting is over. T'is time to bombard editors with article queries in this, a horrible 250th anniversary of the first magazine, as *Discover* and *Health* folded last week.

The Fergie Jenkins project is still on, but I don't think it will go anywhere. He failed to inform me that Putnam's had put out a book on him when he was with Texas. That makes three books that he was associated with in his days. Three books on Fergie Jenkins is all the world needs, I'm sure. But I enjoyed my stint in the Hall of Fame library in Cooperstown, New York doing research on Fergie—until I came across the third book on him. What I really would love to do is a big biography of manager Connie Mack. That would be a piece of work.

Love,

Hank

77. Drew to Nuwer
Lockport, New York
21 August 1991

Dear Hank,

You are in Virginia and Washington, I believe, having some relaxation along with work and a change of scenery and routine. I was pleased with the last letter. The Fergie Jenkins situation seems disappointing.

My reading recently has included some Brian Moore novels, such as *Black Robe, The Doctor's Wife*, and *Lies of Silence*, all very readable though I think he rarely comes up to the earlier *Judith Hearne* and *Catholics*. Also recent books on France and the French called *Fragile Glory* and *Crowns in Conflict*, a kind of group biography of all the European monarchs on the eve of World War I. I've also been interested in the series of John Cheever's journals in *The New Yorker*, which may help cure me of the lingering tendency to confuse John Updike, John Cheever and John Barth.

We have bought an apartment in New York City (really Jim, with a little help from me). This is something he has wanted for forty years and has been working on for the past two years or so. It is a small efficiency in the East Fifties, ninth floor in a pre-war building in good neighborhood (Henry Kissinger, Richard Chamberlain, Myrna Loy, et alii et aliae). I may get up enough energy to go down and resume my decades-ago book-shopping and the like. I spent a lot of time there when Louise Nicholl was living and she had a little office midtown. Sometimes we would commute to her house in Scotch Plains, New Jersey, and sometimes stay in the city in a hotel on Gramercy Park, a fascinating area then.

Love to all,

Bob

78. Drew to Hank
Lockport, New York
17 September 1991

Dear Hank,

This is to report briefly that I survived the [UVM] reunion. It is shocking to see people and to be seen after a fifty-five or sixty year lapse of time, although attempts to recapture old fellowships and intimacies are often quite heart-warming. Fortunately, most of us are rescued from too much nostalgia by our senses of humor, and we did have some good laughs.

I'm reading *God and the Villagers* (Buffalo State Foundation) by a former student, Louis Andrew Vucinich, about his Montenegrin childhood before a harrowing escape from the Nazis brought him here. He married Dr. Mary Cochnower of the English Department, who wrote a learned and very readable background essay on Yugoslavia for the book.

Louis was a big, burly man, gentle as a lamb. Mary was a 17th- century poetry major who was always complaining about drafts and under-heated classrooms. Yet she went to Yugoslavia with Louis when it was not prime tourist territory—the power of love, which can overcome weather and the Cyrillic alphabet and the feuding of Serb and Croat, Macedonian and Albanian, Bosnian and Montenegrin!

It is good that you had some vacation time as a change from your tendency to work a thirty-two hour day, an eight-day week, and a sixty-week year. I'm sure that Adam had a good time.

Though we missed in 1991, we'll make up for it in 1992.

Love,

Bob

79. Drew to Nuwer
Lockport, New York
1 December 1991

The year that brought birthday number 78 in June has been uneventful and pleasant and marked by good health for me and for my co-workers—Jim and the three minpins Sugar, Sionnach and Shadey. I would settle for a similar year in 1992 if I were in a bargaining position.

I have made an ongoing effort to renew or strengthen contact with old college friends from Duke, UVM, Green Mountain and Syracuse but without much success. Buffalo State is closer in space and time. I keep in touch with a number of former colleagues and students both in this area and afar and sometimes run into others in theater lobbies, farmers' markets or restaurants.

The most interesting event of 1991 is the acquisition of a New York City apartment in September. Jim found it after a long search and superintended its refurbishing and furnishing before I went down with him at the end of October for a week. I hadn't gone to New York since before Louise Townsend Nicholl's death ten years ago, though I had made frequent visits in the 1930s, 1940s, 1950s and 1960s. I like the apartment. The building and staff, and the neighborhood very much. We are just across First Avenue from Beekman Place in one of the safest, most attractive and most convenient areas of the city.

On this last visit we had tickets for a spectacular *Aida* at the Met, saw a beautiful Arthurian exhibit at the Public Library, took a three-hour boat ride around Manhattan that I had always missed before, spent an afternoon in the Village, had a look at the New York Marathon, and had amazing luck, an hour after arrival in town, in getting two good seats for Brian Friel's *Dancing at Lughnasa*, which had just opened with the Abbey Theatre company from Dublin.

Hope to see you in 1992. Best from Jim.

Love, Bob

80. Drew to Nuwer
New York, New York
14 April 1992

Dear Hank,

It was good to have a word from you and good news about Hank's mother [released from hospital stay]. I've had two breaks from routine lately—five days in Lockport Memorial Hospital via the 911 paramedics, carried out on a board following a sudden collapse. After catscan, echogram, EKGs and a gallon's worth of "blood work," and IVs and monitors, I was released feeling quite normal and allowed to go to New York City for six days on the train with Jim. Walked across Brooklyn Bridge, but genuinely took it easy. Jim fine.

Love to all, P-Bob

1993 Drew's sixtieth class reunion took place at the University of Vermont.

Again low on money during a freelance writing dry spell, Nuwer accepted an editor position with limited benefits at a struggling arts magazine in Indianapolis. Kurt Vonnegut and Robert Indiana were on the national board of the magazine, but solvency depended on the generosity of Ann Stack, a single major donor who was also the publisher. Essayists Susan Neville and Scott Russell Sanders and writers David Hoppe, Jim Poyser, Ray Begovich, Doug Donaldson, Pat O'Driscoll, Gloria Brame, Jenine Howard Nuwer, Joseph Parisi and Joe Jansen wrote articles or reviews for the magazine.

Nuwer lectured on hazing prevention at a number of colleges.

81. Drew to Nuwer
Lockport, New York
20 February, 1993

Dear Hank,

I am glad that you are going to lecture at the University of Vermont on 22 April. I hope that my "brothers" at the Lambda Iota House (Owls) do not spirit you away and lock you in a deserted silo deep in Chittenden or Lamoille County. If you do have a spare quarter of an hour, drop in at Bailey/Howe Library and speak to the Associate Director for Special Collections, Connell Gallagher, who is a very civilized guy. There are a couple of bronze plaques somewhere memorializing my benefactions in memory of my mother and of my mentor Lester Marsh Prindle and great friend Gladys Gleason Brooks. Don't light any incense lest you run afoul of local indoor pollution regulations.

In front of the venerable Old Mill (cornerstone laid by Lafayette) you'll see the Boulder, symbol of UVM, in front of which I was inducted into Boulder Society with four other senior men in late '32 or early '33—a moment transcending even the junior year Phi Beta Kappa election. Now aren't you sorry you told me?

I think that Connie Gallagher may be the only person at UVM I know in these days. My contemporaries are under sod by now or gibbering in retirement's last stages.

Jim and I had a couple on the Good Saint's day [March 17] in Hertel Avenue's Wellington Pub which tactfully features large flags of the Irish Republic *and* Mother England.

Love to you all,

Bob

82. Drew to Adam Nuwer
Lockport, New York
9 March, 1993

Dear Adam,

(Commenting on this postcard of a shepherd shearing sheep)

This is one of the things I didn't do on any of my trips to England. But I watched sheep being dipped and sheared in the pastures along the sea. In the West the sheep each had a streak of colored dye on their coats to indicate ownership. Green was an O'Malley lamb, red an O'Donnell, blue a McMahon, etc. When I camped out in the Spring, sometimes the lambs would come and nose the tent, or sometimes it would be a cow or even a Connemara pony—nothing wilder, however.

Have a great birthday.

Love to you and your family,

Professor Bob

83. Drew to Nuwer
Buffalo, New York
20 May 1993

Dear Hank,

This paper [letterhead] is pre-Nuwer Buffalo State but to the thrifty Vermonter too good to throw away. It also helps me count my blessings, one of which is not being a department chairperson.

[I'm glad you had] an interesting time [speaking] at the University of Vermont, and I'm happy you liked the place so much. I have always loved both UVM and Duke and been very proud of them. I'm glad you talked with Connie G. and fell afoul of some undergraduate Owls.

The [traditional] potion they mentioned is called Crambambuli, which harks back to the fraternity's founding in 1836 under the "protection" of Lord Byron as a drinking and smoking society. The beverage is prepared annually and is a daunting experience, which I've not had since my thirty-fifth reunion in 1968. One quaffs it only in the sacred precincts to the accompaniment of such songs as "Crambambuli, it is the title of that good drink we love the best; it is the means that proves most vital…" And "Of all the brave birds that ever I see, the Owl is the fairest in her degree…"

Glad you saw some Masefields [in the Drew collection] and a couple of plaques; they owe me a third, for which I plan some arm twisting soon, for the American Literature books and letters given in memory of my old UVM friend Clair Thomas Leonard, a teacher of piano composition, bilingual in French, and a great joy.

Lester Marsh Prindle was UVM '15, a classmate of my great friend Gladys Gleason Brooks, whose story you know. Prindle was a Vermont country boy who made Phi Beta Kappa at the University of Vermont and took his Ph.D. in Latin at Harvard as well as studying in Rome and Athens. He was a dry-looking laconic Vermonter with a wonderful sense of humor. He was chairman of Latin Department (then five people!), and I took a course from him every semester for all four years, majoring in Latin with forty-eight semester hours.

He was tough on me at first, but as soon as I won the Kirby Flower Smith Latin scholarship in a competitive exam I was his boy for good. His wife was a quiet woman of musical tastes and talents; their one son was drowned in Lake Champlain years later. It was a late marriage. I still have a postcard from him in his minuscule hand—his letters were lost, unaccountably. I worked for his classes as I never worked for any others. I think we were very different in personality and teaching performance, but he is my #1 and always has been.

Item: He knew and liked the UVM President Guy W. Bailey, and (I later heard from President Bailey), would go to the President's office and say: "I want you to dig up some more of those little used scholarships. Fraser Drew needs money and can't work any more than he's working now."

And Guy W. would say, "All right, Lester, he can have the Byington scholarship of $200. It's for a student named Byington." Or failing that, a student from Huntington, or failing that, *any* deserving student."

"I'll take it," LMP would answer. "Thank you, Guy. You'll not regret it. *And I'll be back.* Good day."

Good luck in all things as always.

Love to all.

Professor Bob

84. Drew to Nuwer
Buffalo, New York
19 September 1993

Dear Hank,

The good news about the Indiana arts magazine editorship is here, arriving in a beautiful card with the University of Vermont old mill. *Arts Indiana* has some impressive names on its extended masthead, and I hope that it will thrive under your direction. I like the idea of your involvement with such a magazine, and you have Indiana connections.

The lectures at colleges and universities sound good. Your William Paterson talk reminds me that I once was offered the English chair there—back around 1955, I think it was. I very nearly took it but am glad now that I didn't. The president was a delightful lady named Marion Shea, and New York City was close by.

Our new answering machine seems now to be working well. For a time it was completely unreliable, refusing messages or garbling them.

One garbled message contained the word Indiana, and I thought of you—or maybe it was old BSC colleague Frank Hoffman from Nashville, IN.

Love, Bob

1994 *Moment of Truth: Broken Pledges* was shown on NBC as a made-for-TV movie. Nuwer and Eileen Stevens were consultants, Actress Linda Gray played Stevens.

Jim Noble, Nuwer's co-author on the novel-in-progress, died from a heart attack in Missouri, the book dying with him.

85. Drew to Nuwer
Buffalo, New York
28 April 1994

Dear Hank, Jenine, Adam,

Last evening we watched the Richard Nixon funeral. The President's death took me back to Duke University days when he and I were both students there. I did not know him well but liked him. Over the years I saw him and talked with him and Pat in Hartford and in Buffalo when they were campaigning. The letters from them both I gave to the University of Vermont's library quite a few years ago. The pictures he sent, inscribed as U.S. Senator, a Vice-President, and later as President are framed and hung on the walls here. The last of the three is signed by both Nixon and Pat, and she looks lovely in a pink dress. She was a nice lady. Europeans seem to feel that we made too much of Watergate and lost a President who was a genius at foreign policy. Although I have been for some time a liberal Democrat I tend to disagree. If you are Nixonphobes, you can just ascribe this to incipient senility on my part.

I was angry to find that I do not have Channel 11, on which your *Broken Pledges* was shown. I switched channels madly, but with no luck. Let me know how it went and what reactions you had.

It was good to hear the excellent news that Jenine and Adam are joining Hank on the banks of the Wabash.

Love to all, Professor Bob

86. Drew to Nuwer
Buffalo, New York
25 July, 1994

Dear Jenine and Hank,

According to the *Literary Book of Days*, an often used gift from the Nuwers, on this day in 1856, Charles Major, author of *When Knighthood Was in Flower*, was born in Indianapolis. You will please me by making no reference to Coach Bobby [Knight].

…[Former English Professor] Dr. Eloise N. Courter sends regards to Hank. She was with the Sherwins, Jim and me at Dr. Julia C. Piquette's house [emeritus Buffalo State professor of communication and English] for a very good birthday dinner on 23 June. Eloise also has a June birthday.

At long last I wrote memoirs of Louise Townsend Nicholl and I. L. Salomon, underrated poets and good friends to Jim and me. The UVM Library journal *Liber* will publish the Nicholl piece [and later the Salomon piece]…

No more now.

Love to you *all*.

Bob

87. Nuwer to Drew
Middletown, Indiana
Christmas Day, 1994

Dear Professor Bob:

I was thrilled to see you get some deserved kudos from Buffalo State in an alumni publication.

It has been very, very busy. The commute from Middletown, Indiana, near Muncie, takes up to two hours and twenty minutes a day all told, plus the usual 60-plus hour weeks in the office. The good staff has had a kind of tough time with a magazine devoted to the arts finding enough subscribers to keep it afloat. Sales to new subscribers have been disappointing, and there is no telling how long the main backer will go with her gifts. Keep your fingers crossed that I can use the *Arts Indiana* editorship to move into another position. This job has no benefits and no retirement. I will try to help my cause by working even more hours in Indianapolis, teaching an arts journalism specialty course for the Indiana University School of Journalism. I also agreed to speak at the Society of Professional Journalists' convention in Nashville, Tennessee next March.

Thanks for remembering Adam at Christmas, and give Jim our best.

Love,

Hank

1995 Nuwer's *How to Write Like an Expert About Anything* was a book-of-the month selection from Writer's Digest Books.

Nuwer taught arts reporting in the spring for his boss James W. Brown of the Indiana University School of Journalism at the IUPUI campus and would remain connected to IUPUI until his retirement in 2008.

Nuwer published an *Arts Indiana* essay on Drew called "Under the Influence: My Powerful Mentor." With *Arts Indiana* failing to find enough arts-loving subscribers and about to fail, Hank accepted a visiting associate position at the University of Richmond in Virginia. He taught with a distinguished crew, including Mike Spear, a former copy editor and grandson of author Sherwood Anderson; Steve Nash, a sometimes freelance journalist for the *Washington Post*, and Hal Wingo, a former *Life* magazine war correspondent who partnered with the late photographer Larry Burrows.

88. Nuwer to Drew
Middletown, Indiana
February 9, 1995

Dear Professor Drew:

Hope this note finds you well and looking forward to the imminent arrival of trilliums and crocuses. It has been very hectic. I finished *How to Write Like an Expert* for Writer's Digest Books. I also am teaching a class in arts reporting at Indiana University, Purdue University Indianapolis (IUPUI). I have been working double forty hours for a long time. Circulation stays low for *Arts Indiana*, and I put a tremendous amount of time into the publication.

We only have three full-time people on the magazine. With turnover, I have even had to put out the January issue alone. Your note regarding my essay "Open Arms Motel" cheered me. Let's hope some other readers discover the magazine. I received fifteen reader letters about "Open Arms." That is a very high percentage. I was gratified.

With the magazine's future uncertain I reluctantly keep an eye out for any jobs that have retirement and health benefits. In the meantime, I throw my efforts wholeheartedly into *Arts Indiana.*

I loved your memoir on Louise T. Nicholl since she is the poet whose book you awarded me after the Contemporary Literature class in 1968. She has a special place in my past life.

Love,

Hank

89. Drew to Nuwer
Buffalo, New York
29 March 1995

Dear Hank and Jenine:

Arts Indiana Volume 17, Number 3 here and green-covered and beautiful. Am going to read Susan Neville's piece on author Marguerite Young and the others today, but I wished to get a note off at once.

I'm delighted all over again by Hank's article about his mentor. This issue will one day be fought over by collectors. Extra copies are most welcome, but I know that they do not grow free on the banks of the Wabash. I enclose check for extras. I want to give one to the president of Buffalo State, F.C. Richardson, who is under a lot of fire right now but is a good man.

Love to all Nuwers,

Bob

90. Drew to Nuwer
Buffalo, New York
16 April 1995

Dear Hank

Just now, late morning of Easter Sunday, I telephoned a lady I have been intending to call for a long time. Before I could wish her a Happy Easter, she answered the phone by saying, "Happy Easter." Your mother and I had a good visit, Hank, and we discovered that I am six years ahead of her in age. We also expressed disbelief that Adam could already be ten years old. We also talked about THE article—"Under the Influence: My Powerful Mentor."

Thus, the April *Arts Indiana* continues to occupy the stage. I sent one to former President Paul Bulger, and he and his wife were delighted with it. He has macular degeneration and is legally blind, but Marion read the article to him, and he printed a brief response on a card: "Hank Nuwer's article is beautiful. What a great tribute to a professor! And so say I…Marion says you have always been handsome! Love, Paul and Marion."

Copies have gone out, along with, I confess, several photocopies, which is probably illegal. I am hoping that my connection with the editor in chief will keep me from getting into trouble. Kevin Starr, English teacher at Clarence High and a top student at BSC, wrote: "Thank you for the copy of Hank Nuwer's piece…I find him very readable and his images riveting, especially when he is describing you." Edna Lindemann, the retired founder of the Burchfield Center at BSC, wrote: "…I can only tell you, my elegant colleague, that I adore Hank Nuwer for what he recognized in you, learned from you, and applied." Marvin LaHood who, has been nominated for Distinguished Teaching Professor, was happy with the article for your writing, your appreciation of me, his close friend.

He would agree, I'm sure, that I never taught you anything. You are completely your own writer. What I did was to offer sincere interest, appreciation, encouragement.

Jim reassembled our fountain, emptied and wrapped for the winter, before he left for New York. It has burbled on through these cold nights, facing the light each morning with icicles and looking like one of Robert Frost's spring brooks or pools. The wind remains cold off the lake.

Love to you all,

Bob

91. Drew to Nuwer
Buffalo, New York
20 April 1995

Big envelope of *Arts Indianas* [with essay on Drew] came yesterday and is appreciated and will be put to good use. I sent one at once to Ernest Boyer, the SUNY chancellor who initiated the [SUNY] Distinguished Teaching Professor rank and presented the first group of promotions (9) in 1973. He is now head of the Carnegie Endowment for the Advancement of Teaching in Princeton, New Jersey. I touch base with him every year or two and like seeing him on TV.

My high school Latin & French teacher in senior year (her first job at 21, fresh out of Lester Marsh Prindle's classes at the University of Vermont) wrote about the "beautifully written article." She said, "I am glad you are receiving recognition for your teaching while you are still around to enjoy it. One can never be sure of appropriate elegies." She enclosed a snapshot taken on my senior class ride to the White Mountains, New Hampshire in 1929. "Can you remember that trip 66 years ago? A little scary, isn't it. I was only 21 years old, you not quite 16. Apparently we were wearing belts very low that year, and your white knickers are pretty `cool,' too. My diary says that we had a wonderful day, and that's how I remember it."

On back of the picture of herself and me she had written, "June 11, 1929. Senior class ride to White Mountains. I rode with Fraser Drew and Margaret DuBois."

The article reached Garth Jeffers [one of the twin sons of the Carmel, California poet Robinson Jeffers] just as he and Brenda were leaving on a cruise to Canary Islands, Casablanca, Civitavecchia, Lisbon, Isle of Guernsey, London, Dublin—followed by time in Munich and Paris, home June 19. Quick note praised the "excellent" and "interesting" article and Hank Nuwer's "real admiration." I wanted [Garth] to see the Robinson Jeffers mentions, especially. He ends, "Brenda joins me in sending much affection."

Other compliments on the article have come from Masefield authority Crocker Wight, a member of the Board of Overseers of Harvard University.

Love to all,

Bob.

92. Drew to Nuwer
Buffalo, New York
7 May 1995

Dear Hank,

Sunday morning and wonderful fresh spring air in the upper fifties. Yesterday's News had the obituary of Charles A. Brady, 83, longtime English chair at Canisius College and book reviewer for the *Buffalo News*, author of four novels and several other books. In my early Buffalo years I saw Charles and his wife Eileen often and audited his classes whenever I could leave Buffalo State long enough to hear him. He was an extremely learned man and an exciting lecturer.

Another response to the Mentor article came from Doris Kerns Eddins, a dear lady who supervised elementary teachers. Her husband Lloyd used to play basketball for State. "I have read the article three times. It is delightful. Did you really hold the baby? I'll bet it was the first time you ever held anyone who tried to wriggle out of your arms. I must say that you taught your students to write well."

I have difficulty keeping a straight face when some reactor gives me credit for your writing, Hank. It is as if you reported after class for three consecutive days for a shot of Professor Drew's secret formula and two teaspoons of his elixir. On the fourth day he pressed your button three times and you took off on a successful career. If only it were that simple and uncomplicated and quick, huh?

Hey, it's lunchtime. The dogs will join me in an attentive half circle like wolves leering around a fire.

Love,

Bob

93. Nuwer to Drew
Richmond, Virginia
December 18, 1995

Dear Professor Bob:

The last year I've thought quite a bit about a Basque sheepherder I interviewed in 1978. Bernard Tristent lived in a Buffalo, Wyoming hotel named the Idlewild. It had a clientele of herders, retirees from ranch life and guys like me who stayed for a week or two before drifting with the tumbleweeds east or west. Fifty, Tristent's legs due to multiple sclerosis had collapsed on him like trees rotted from within. He hadn't saved much. Doctor's bills took what little he had, but the owner of the Idlewild let him stay rent-free to keep an eye on the other lodgers. At least that's what he was told and it gave him a sense of dignity.

Tristent approached me because he wanted his story on tape. The recorder and the fact an outsider, a reporter, was listening somehow gave the events of his life legitimacy. His poverty and the fact he had no relatives in America made it unlikely he'd get a grave marker as death approached. Having his name in a magazine wasn't as significant as having his name on a gravestone in a cemetery with all the other Basques who died in America, but it was better than death followed by oblivion.

I find myself looking at fifty next year. I'd like to think my best creative work awaits me. I've been writing personal essays that may form a complete memoir one day, putting them down on paper when not making lesson plans and finishing the new book on hazing for Indiana University Press.

I continue to write. *How to Write Like an Expert* came out last September for Writer's Digest Books, my title changed against my advice by editors and the sales crew to the awful and pretentious *How to Write Like an Expert About Anything.*

Jenine and Adam fly to Richmond from Indiana on the 24th of December. We'll decorate the tree that night and put the old Lionel train set from 1950 together the next day. Weather permitting we'll go bike riding during the visit.

Love,

Hank

1996 Nuwer stepped up his writing of *At the Crest*, a history of Cedar Crest College.

94. Nuwer to Drew
Richmond, Virginia
March 15, 1996

Dear Professor Bob and Jim:

Wish I could raise a St. Patrick's Day glass with you.

All is ok here. I will continue to commute to Richmond from Indiana until May 1997. The school gave me another one-year contract. I am working on the Cedar Crest College history book now. I'll see Jenine and Adam this weekend.

Love,

Hank

95. Drew to Nuwer
Buffalo, New York
26 March, 1996

Dear Hank,

It is the birthday of A. E. Housman and Robert Frost.

We are still having snow and winter, but in this neighborhood everything looks beautiful—from inside, to the non-driver! Last week was spring-like and I had begun to take little, tentative walks down the block to Elmwood Avenue, where there is a bank, and up to Bryant and home. To the old bones after the inactivity of winter, that is a good walk.

I am delighted that Richmond renewed you for a year. They seem to recognize a good man when they have one. But I suppose it is virtually impossible for you to find any time for writing, teaching being the jealous mistress that she is. Time was always so difficult to find, and now when I have much of it on my hands I prefer curling up on my couch with a warm dog or two to any strenuous mental or physical activity.

Love,

Bob

96. Nuwer to Drew
Middletown, Indiana
August 1, 1996

Dear Professor Bob:

I hope you are enjoying a productive and peaceful summer. I also hope that your health is good, the humidity in Buffalo is at a record low, and that a statue has been erected in your honor in front of Ketchum Hall. If the last two have failed to occur, I hope your health is great nonetheless. I am hard at work on the new book on hazing for Indiana University Press. This project consumes me at present.

One other book I wish to write in my lifetime is a collection of nonfiction essays, and the fact that my personal hero in life is St. Augustine may give you some insight into content. I do want to include the essay on you, "My Powerful Mentor," that *Arts Indiana* published.

My summer has been productive and most hectic. I had hoped for the former, not the latter. "Hectic" aptly describes any freelancer's life. *Harper's Magazine* reprinted a section from *Broken Pledges* and I contributed to a small article in the *New York Times Sunday Magazine*. I also agreed to participate as a hazing expert in an educational film.

With Jenine's blessing I have begun home schooling Adam. The curriculum includes Latin (We began with Caesar), history (Roman so far), science (he has challenged creation theories), math (algebra and geometry), geography (his favorite, and he is a whiz at Trivial Pursuit!), grammar (English and Latin simultaneously), and literature. So far we've read selections from *Lives of a Cell* by Lewis Thomas. *Refuge* by Terry Tempest Williams, *Maus: A Survivor's Tale* by Art Spiegelman—which he loved, short stories by Jack London and William Carlos Williams, and two Mark Twain novels, *Tom Sawyer* and *Huckleberry Finn.*

The arrangement has not only been beneficial for Adam but helpful for me as a person and writer to review material I once loved—and to gain mastery in recent biology and post-1980 history. It has extinguished all social life and correspondence as you have noticed. But the rewards far eclipse any hardship. Adam whistles and laughs and jokes again, and what a blessing that is. When he's ready he'll rejoin the public school system, but he has no timetable he must meet. Adam and I leave Jenine and Indiana about August 5 for our new home in Virginia.

At the University of Richmond I teach great subjects: journalism law and ethics, arts reporting, creative nonfiction writing (including the *old* "New Journalism"), and publications management. I'm getting a good grasp of the Internet and have a real interest in using it for research and journalism.

Two unsettling things happened at the University of Richmond last year. One, a thief or thieves removed my computer and several other Macs on my office floor by breaking down a door and then removing paneling from the ceiling to flit from room to room. I lost the notes to one interview with a dean at Northern Illinois University for the hazing book, but I can transcribe again. My biggest losses were my entire memoir through age thirty-five and nearly all my lesson plans. Yes, I know better to back up. The first thing my mother with an eighth-grade education said when I called her about the theft was this: "Did you make copies?" I told my nearest neighbor in Middletown whose truck tires, I think, stand thirty-one feet tall and who holds the world's record in the loud muffler event; he said this: "You mean you didn't back everything up—how come?"

The intruders wanted Macs—period. The thieves ignored spare change, a Waterman pen in case, very expensive leather portfolios with my life's magazine and newspaper publications in them, and signed first-edition books by Booth Tarkington and other authors.

The second bad thing was that my boss had a blood clot during "routine" knee surgery and nearly died two weeks ago. It was a very close call for my boss Mike Spear. Mike's been a supporter of my writing for a decade, and I'm grateful he came through. I was in Virginia with Mike a day after his knee surgery for an injury he sustained in a faculty-student softball game. Though he said he had "indigestion," he was showing me his rare first editions and signed books and manuscripts from Frost, Jeffers, Sherwood Anderson— his grandfather—and many more authors. That night his wife rushed him to an emergency room and saved his life.

It turns out that he had always had clotting problems, but he neglected to discuss this with his doctor before the operation. I wish, in view of my failure to back up my memoir and the lesson plans, I could tell you I resisted badgering him about this, but ask I did. "How come, Mike?" Must be my mother's influence.

On to my hazing book research for Indiana University Press.

I plan to spend much of August taking Adam through the Smithsonian and the Library of Congress. There we'll visit with Bob

Waite, my friend from Idaho who works in Washington for the Justice Department. I haul my hazing book files from Virginia to Indiana and back in the camper of my truck as easily as if they were paperbacks in a briefcase.

Thanks for reading, Professor Bob. I hope, like me, you are excited about the next hazing book and its implications for reform of student organizations such as fraternities and sororities.

Adam is writing you a thank you for the gingerbread cake you sent last December. We took it out of the freezer and put it together yesterday. It was still edible.

Love,

Hank

97. Drew to Nuwer
Buffalo, New York
18 October 1996

Dear Hank,

Not much happens here. Jim had a wonderful fortnight in Paris. He liked it better than the other big cities he has seen and found the French unexpectedly warm and helpful. He looked up Shakespeare and Company, the bookshop where Joyce and Hemingway used to browse [ed. at another locale] and borrow, and brought me the French version of *A Moveable Feast* which I am reading to scrape some of the rust off my University of Vermont minor in French.

We have a third dog again to "replace" Sugar who died last November. This is 3-month-old, 3-pound Fawn (maybe it should be Faun?), a Chihuahua whom we have had three days and find amazingly bright and resourceful. The miniature pinchers tolerate her and gain respect for her. I wonder how I managed a Newfoundland, a German shepherd, a Doberman.

I am deafer, creakier, more inclined to solitude but still in operation.

Love to you all, Bob

98. Drew to Nuwer and Other Friends
Buffalo, New York
November 30, 1996

The *Michael Collins* film with Liam Neeson which I saw on its first afternoon in Buffalo took me back to many visits to Dublin and the west of County Cork in the 1960's and 1970's. Especially it took me back to 13 June, 1971 when I attended a memorial service for Collins held in the Church of the Most Holy Trinity in the grounds of Dublin Castle.

Of all the Free State or Pro–Treaty party of the 1920's in Irish politics, Michael Collins made the greatest appeal to the imagination, although my allegiance was always to the Republican side and its leaders like Éamon de Valera, Constance Markiewicz*, Cathal Brugha** and Harry Boland***, whose political party took the name Fianna Fáil. Perhaps time will eventually place de Valera and Collins side by side as friends and co-leaders of the fight for Irish freedom, one tragically killed at 31, the other the survivor of many struggles to die at 93.

On 16 August 1967 my friend Jim Brophy and I had the privilege of an hour's talk with Éamon de Valera in the president's office at the [official residence] Àras an Uachtarain in Phoenix Park.

The closest I could come to Michael Collins was a memorial service held almost forty-nine years after his death (on 22 August 1922). This service, a late morning solemn high military Mass, was attended by members of the Collins family, veterans who had worked and fought beside Collins in the six years following the Easter Rising of 1916, their children and grandchildren, and members of Fine Gael, the political party which had evolved from supporters of the Treaty with Britain, the followers of Michael Collins and Arthur Griffith.

I had no right to be present at the service beyond that of an Irish-American deeply interested in the Irish history of the 1916-1932 years. I arrived early and talked with *Gardai* [Irish police force known as Guardians of the Peace of Ireland] at the entrance to the Castle Grounds. On my month-long visits to Ireland in the Sixties and Seventies I traveled light. My every-day costume often included black shoes, black trousers and a black trenchcoat, which, I discovered to my surprise and amusement, frequently misidentified me as a visiting priest from the States, especially in the small towns of the Irish south and West. I rarely pointed out this error and was in no hurry to discard its advantages of special courtesies. On this day at Dublin Castle the *Gardai* probably accepted me as a friendly American priest, and I joined the memorial crowd unchallenged.

The service was just under an hour in length, impressive and moving. In the throng I saw perhaps the only other two other persons who were not Fine Gael adherents. One was a military man in uniform, the personal representative of the President of Ireland, Éamon de Valera. The other was the Prime Minister and the head of Fianna Fáil, then as often in the years since 1932 the majority party in the Irish government. Jack Lynch, who was Taoiseach from 1966 to 1973 and from 1977 to 1979, was a skilled and charismatic leader. After the Mass I got a good picture of him, cool and debonair with his pipe and homburg, in a crowd of his political opposition. The military ceremony in the courtyard was fascinating, and I was moved by the sight of the veterans, men in their seventies and eighties marching in their old uniforms and carrying the guns and the tattered banners of a half-century before.

That night in my hotel room jut off St. Stephen's Green, I read a 1961 paperback biography of Michael Collins purchased at a book stall on my walk back from Dublin Castle. Today I took the book down again from a bookshelf in my home in Buffalo. The well-worn cover is two-thirds occupied by a drawing of Collins in uniform over the caption, "The Big Fellow. He gave his life in the struggle for Irish independence." The strong face of Michael Collins in the drawing is uncannily like that of Liam Neeson in the film.

Bob

*Ed. Constance Markiewicz was a Fianna Fáil political leader and feminist.

**Ed. Brugha was an Irish revolutionary seriously wounded in the Easter 1916 uprising.

***Ed. Harry Boland, politician shot by Free State national Army members.

99. Nuwer to Drew
Richmond, Virginia
February 2, 1997

Dear Professor Bob:

I hope you are finding 1997 to be a kind and peaceful year. It's fun to think of months the way we think of dogs' lives in comparison to human lifespans. Each month would be the equivalent to seven or ten years in human years. 1997 should reach adulthood in March. We'll see its character unfold, and we'll despair that it ever will turn out ok. But it probably will somehow.

I hope your body gives you more good days than bad. If you need me to locate an article or book for you, you need only drop a postcard. You've done so much for me. If you had not entered my life I would be writing smug silly satires and turning out adventure novels by the dozen. You gave me a base of learning and a perspective, plus you had the patience to wait while I erred and explored, offering only positive reinforcement at the right time.

You and an old Little League coach of mine, Steve Bania, a former minor league baseball player, gave me the strong male role models that I needed in addition to the love I got from my father. Your support has gotten me through life, and I hope I am giving that same kind of role model support to Adam and Chris and my students, male and female.

I have come to the sad conclusion that my Dad must have suffered a type of traumatic stress disorder during World War Two (I wouldn't dare suggest this to my mother!), when his best friend was blown up while they were eating rations together in the shade of their tank, a tank they named Lonely. He tried his very best, but he couldn't relate to using one's mind to make a living, perhaps because his own father had forbidden him to attend high school in 1928 or 1929.

My schedule continues to be hectic. I pulled two all-nighters last week but managed to get ten hours of sleep Thursday night and six hours last night so I'm fine. Preparations for each University of Richmond law and ethics class take me from four to six hours, but it's a wonderful learning opportunity. My magazine management class is launching an online magazine, certainly a pioneer experiment in college publications. Some day no one will read anything in print. It will all be digital and on a screen.

Adam continues to do well on his home schooling. He's made one great friend here. It's been wonderful for me to return to my Latin training as I teach him.

We have science experiments all over the house. He's testing the fish tank for ammonia, PH, hardness. We have crystals growing in the living room in plastic containers. He has a nightlight over a jar in the living room to hatch his brine shrimp. It's so peaceful here and nice.

Somewhat of a distraction is that Dorothy Gulbenkian Blaney, the president of Cedar Crest College, is putting pressure on Cedar Crest alumnae, publisher of the history I have completed, to suppress the manuscript, primarily because the school's president and board admitted in a board meeting to giving its faculty bogus graduate degrees and undergraduates bogus degrees at times from 1893 through 1926.*

The commonwealth of Pennsylvania did not give permission to give these degrees, but the old College did it anyway. This fact being made known upsets Dr. Blaney, but since she is paid $249,000 a year, and I get $10,000 for nearly a decade's work for the history, I think (smile) she can endure a truthful history of a truly great college for women.

The Cedar Crest history is a benefit to my life. One of its alums was a Japanese woman of American descent stuck in Japan during World War Two. One of my young adult books not yet written will be a fictionalized account of a young American family marooned in Japan during the war. If possible I will combine research for this trip with a trip to the Philippines to study fraternity hazing/brutality there, plus whatever scholarship I can locate on Japanese-Americans toiling under Hideki Tojo. Maybe I'll pay homage to Ernie Pyle, killed near Okinawa at Ie Shima by a sniper's shot to the head.

Anyway, if that Japanese-American alum could tolerate so much misery, certainly I can put up with any piddling problems I have.

I have one week ahead to proofread my *The Legend of Jesse Owens* book due out in September nationwide.

The sad thing is that an old friend from the University of Nevada calls me in the middle of the night trudging out what he thinks are *my* grievances against University of Nevada faculty from the 1970s and expects me to rail. The fact is I've either forgotten or forgiven slights, or seen what I then perceived to be someone else's fault as my own flaws. Going for a Ph.D. in a program then heavy on literary criticism was a bad decision, but back then who knew you could get an M.F.A elsewhere in creative writing, especially in creative nonfiction?

Speaking of creative writing, I have finished John Gardner's *On Moral Fiction*. If your eyes again permit reading you would love this book, I think. Jenine bought me two nice first editions by Gardner as early Valentine's Day presents. Did you ever read Gardner's fiction? His essays appeal to me also. Some of his fanciful fiction smacks of too much invention, too little character, as does the worst of Kurt Vonnegut.

I have two of the greatest colleagues at the University of Richmond anyone could ever want. Both Steve Nash and Mike Spear have written a lot, love students, and care about quality instruction. I'll miss the University of Richmond, as close to a home as a teacher I have ever had. My boss, Mike Spear, grandson of Sherwood Anderson, has recovered completely from his brush with death from a blood clot last year.

Adam has become the mascot of journalism's Ryland Hall. He chats up everyone, and few in the student union think it strange any longer that there is a kid sipping a Dr Pepper and reading his Latin text, or an abridged *Don Quixote*, or Steinbeck's *Of Mice and Men*.

Off the topic—Jenine gave me an antique burlap and leather Inuit salmon creel. She cleaned it up herself. It's the best bookbag I've ever had.

Also, I am thinking of willing or even donating all my signed correspondence from James Dickey, David Mamet, Vonnegut and so on to Buffalo State.

Onward and upward.

Love,

Hank

*Ed. At the Crest was published in spite of Dr. Blaney's misgivings, thanks to the perseverance of Heidi Butler and her alumnae publications committee at Cedar Crest College. Dr. Blaney died after a long fight with cancer in 2006. The history was well received by CCC alums and caused no controversy.

100. Nuwer to Drew
Richmond, Virginia
February 28, 1997

Dear Professor Bob:

Received the sad news of the passing of my Aunt Marion, my lovely godmother. My aunt was always a spoiler, making me rhubarb treats, and I was glad I was able to dedicate *How to Write Like an Expert* to her in 1995.

Adam is reading three books a week for home schooling. He now is reading *White Fang* by Jack London.

Love,

Hank

101. Nuwer to Drew
Anderson Indiana
August 19, 1997

Dear Professor Bob:

Jenine, Adam and I took a trip to the Upper Peninsula of Michigan. We stayed in a wonderful hunting lodge that had great red cedar logs. It was featured in a hunting article in *Life* many years ago under the description of "millionaire's cabin."

Naturally, I took a Hemingway pilgrimage to Seney and fished the Fox River and reread "Big Two-Hearted River" by Hemingway.

Surprisingly, all the grasshoppers here are black. I wonder if they are black because nature made them that way, not because their food supply was burned" as Hemingway perhaps erroneously wrote in "Big Two-Hearted River."

Today is my birthday, fifty-one.

Love,

Hank

102. Drew to Nuwer
Buffalo, New York
26 August, 1997

Dear Hank:

I was glad to hear you had been "Up in Michigan." If I hadn't gone on that three-decade Irish binge, I'd probably have gone to the Hemingway places, at least to Paris, Venice, Key West, Idaho and Michigan—and perhaps to Spain but probably not East Africa. Well, I did get to Havana and Hemingway himself, and I still re-live that visit and marvel at his kindness and the on-going correspondence.

Black grasshoppers in the Upper Peninsula! The Vermont ones were green and gold, like the state and university colors.

Love,

Bob

103. Nuwer to Drew
Anderson, Indiana
September 1, 1997

Dear Professor Bob:

Be alert! Some forger has taken your letterhead stationery and is writing to me.

I don't have to be mystery sleuth Dorothy Sayers to spot the forgery.

The minute that I read that Fraser Drew, unaccompanied by Jim Brophy, had opened his doors to the citizenry of Greater Buffalo for a house tour I knew the letter was a fake.

I have just mentioned your home tour to Jenine. As soon as she revives she undoubtedly will have a comment.

Actually, I think it's marvelous. I admire anyone with the courage to face an oncoming herd. If I gave a home tour it would be, ahem, a "tour de farce."

An English department head at Ball State called and asked if I wanted to teach two courses in composition beginning the next day. I guess they had an instructor drop out or an overload. I decided not to teach. It would have been torture for the class and me. I'm not good at winging.

My old Ball State friend Dr. Louis Ingelhart had a double blow. He had lost his wife Margaret to cancer and now he fell off his porch in Muncie, breaking his arm. He's in a health center nearby undergoing therapy. I brought him a news magazine Saturday and will get some nice fruit today.

It's weird to hear this young snip of a therapist talking to Ingelhart—this cultured, feisty First Amendment champion—as if he were a baby, calling him "Louis."

He's still a fierce warrior. She'd better not turn her back. If he gets mad she'll be wearing a bedpan for headgear.

Love,

Hank

104. Drew to Nuwer
Buffalo, New York
September 7, 1997

Dear Hank,

Your letter was very funny. But please re-read mine. I couldn't have told you I opened my HOUSE to the unwashed—or even well-scrubbed—multitude. Never in a million years. The dogs would have raised hell and welts on intruding calves and thighs. I would have had to nail shut the library-study door.

It was the GARDEN that was open to the slavering public, via the east gate. Even the courtyard was not included. Hordes peeped over the east and south brick walls to see the fountain and the espaliered ginkgos and the occasional bathing bird. I still have not recovered from the strain of outside graciousness from ten a.m. to four p.m. Inside, never. But the letter was fun, anyhow.

Your friend Dr. Ingelhart has had a rough time all right, and then to listen to the first-naming and patronizing of the therapist! I love the thought of her "wearing a full bed pan" and immediately fashioned a list of people I would love to see so decorated—it's the "Who's Who in Bed Pans."

On another note, I liked your "Outsiders*." They're brisk, but unhurried, something I would have liked to try. But I'm a little heavy for that as a column and wouldn't have been able to cut them off neatly at 600 or 700 words.

Keep me informed.

I am working some Druid spells in connection with your job situation. Drew is from O'Draoi, *draoi* being Irish Gaelic for a druid. I make our big beech nervous just walking around it. But don't expect much. I don't work much magic for myself.

Love,

Bob

Ed. Nuwer has begun writing a for-fun weekly hunting and fishing column called "The Outsider" for the Muncie Star-Press.

105. Drew to Nuwer
Buffalo, New York
22 December, 1997

Dear *Famille* Nuwer:

Two envelopes here from you. There was much news in these pieces of communication. I'm glad to be in touch with your various activities. I continue to be amazed by your individual and collective activities.

Caroline Heyman of BSC Art is 100 and sent a holiday letter. Some losses in the old BSC community. Hank may remember Hertha S. Ganey, who brought a deep knowledge of both ancient and contemporary literature to her teaching of children's literature. She looked like one's pie-baking grandmother and could fight like a tiger. She died well into her nineties.

Hank may also have known Eugene Dakin of Art and Theatre, another of those big, bright, bearded men with a bright, beautiful wife. Do I need to name another?

I met Gene & Penny Dakin one summer years ago on the main street of Randolph, Vermont, my hometown, to the surprise of us all. Thereafter, whenever Gene and I met, he would lift me high in the air and ask, "How's the Randolph Flash?"

Gene Dakin died four years ago. Penny, his wife, was matriarch of the Democratic Party and often ran for office in republican Kenmore when no one else would. She was known for sending a single red rose to congratulate or to thank or to comfort. In late November I wrote her a letter for her 78th birthday, aware that she was very ill. A week later a single red rose arrived with a small card, "Love ya, Penny." Day before yesterday I attended her funeral. It was the last rose she had sent.

Love from Bob

1998 Franklin Watts published Nuwer's biography on Jesse Owens.

106. Drew to Nuwer
Buffalo, New York
10 May 1998

Dear Hank, Jenine and Adam (and Chris if...on premises)

I am happy to hear of the contract for a book on high school hazing. A survey of your books and articles would certainly not reveal a narrowness of subject matter.

The Nuwer bell, which tolls and tinkles in my mind frequently, has been ringing all day because I just packed your books and other publications marked Nuwer 3rd floor #10. I really never believed that I would move again until the time came for incineration and shipment to the quiet hillside in Vermont. The new place is ours, but we have to sell this one. And so I have begun packing books and papers. Already boxed, with Nuwers, are Irish-American [writers], Buffalo writers, an interesting container of [Mary] Renault, [C.P.] Cavafy, [Lawrence] Durrell and ancient Greeks, a run of *Eire-Ireland* from [issue] I in 1965 to 1995, and French and Roman literature from the *Satyricon* to the *Little Prince*. I am slowed by arthritis, nostalgia, and rediscovery.

The new place we are buying with friend Mutsuo Tomita, who is very fond of Buffalo and will visit frequently. It is a condo on the riverfront with wonderful views to north, west and south—an end unit with attached neighbors only on the east. I am to have sole possession of the 3rd or top floor, to which I will travel on the elevator. In recent months the beautiful staircase here has been a torment because of a back-and-leg problem which a therapist-chiropractor is helping.

Portside is part of the Buffalo Waterfront Village. Our unit is one of its four largest and is directly on the water. Each of the three floors has a terrace looking southwest—nice sunsets, though I don't plan much terrace time in winter months! Condo is only nine years old with one owner, a [physician] from Roswell Park [Cancer Institute] now gone to Ohio. It is in excellent shape and is 3400 square feet with three bedrooms, three-and-a-half baths.

I'd best go back to packing, but I wanted you to know. I'll send full address, phone, etc. as M[oving] Day approaches.

Love to all,

Bob

107. Nuwer to Drew
Anderson, Indiana
December 15, 1998

Dear Professor Bob:

Happy holidays from the Nuwers. Don't pay the ransom. We haven't been kidnapped, just insanely busy. Hence not much correspondence lately. I teach (adjunct) a couple places, complete the new hazing book, freelance articles and take care of Adam. Mostly, it has been the hazing book that has kept me chained.

Your cheery Christmas letter was read and reread. We will be in Buffalo at Christmas briefly to visit my mother. If you would like visitors for a brief hour to show off your new dwelling, let us know. We will visit Chris and his wife Susan the night of December 26th in Ann Arbor.

I am sending some literary goodies such as John Masefield reading copies in this package. Sending Masefield to Drew is like sending a crucifix to my mother in overkill. But I thought that since you had sent your Masefields to the University of Vermont that perhaps some night by the fire you might long to reread one of your departed volumes. Voila! You walk over to your shelves and haul out *Thanks Before Going* and *The Everlasting Mercy* and satisfy that craving.

Jenine is in Chicago at a conference. She and her dad in Chicago stole away to attend a Robert Capa exhibition of photographs. Capa at the end of World war Two had been shooting in Germany. Mr. Howard, Jenine's dad, always had said that a *Life* photographer had snapped his picture in Germany. Alas, none of the pictures were of him or his war buddies, but the settings were familiar to him. Jenine said she thought of you when she saw Capa's Ernest Hemingway and Gary Cooper shots in Idaho.

I hope your health continues to be good.

My sad news is that Joe Nikiel, former Buffalo State alumni president and my friend of forty-one years, passed away in November at fifty-three. We were in Boy Scouts together in Cheektowaga Troop 54. He was a school superintendent and a lovely guy. This death was another devastating loss of a friend.

My old partner, photographer Max Aguilera Hellweg, is taking medical studies at Trinity College in Dublin. Max had a great cover spread on medical advances in *Life Magazine* two issues back.

Work goes well on the young adult nonfiction books. The good news is that I have another contract for a Scholastic book on high school hazing. Who would have guessed this would become my specialty?

I am pondering writing an author biography for my next project, maybe Booth Tarkington. The other biography of Tarkington was done in the Fifties by James Woodress, older brother of journalist and former Ball State colleague Fred Woodress.

James Woodress was a visiting professor at Duke University when his "Booth Tarkington: Gentleman from Indiana" came out. Woodress had the cooperation of the last Mrs. Tarkington, who allowed him to use Tarkington's papers at Princeton. The biography is one-sided and peppy and, well, banal, so as to be unreadable now.

James Woodress said in the introduction that he meant for the biography to be a paean to Tarkington so that new generations of Americans might read him. Alas, a critical biography might have done more justice to Newton Booth Tarkington. Perhaps Woodress felt he needed to take a tone of homage and obeisance to get Mrs. T's cooperation—a case, I can't resist, of "no paean, no gain."

Sorry. Did you just crumble the letter in disgust, Professor Bob?

The other author I am considering for a biography is Kurt Vonnegut.

Give me a call at my mother's either late December 23 or anytime December 24 if you'd like company. The last time you saw Adam he was two. Now he's a sharp thirteen-year-old, a lover of *Star Trek* and fishing and bad puns and jokes.

I still read to Adam. We read Jack London's funny story about Spot the dog, and Adam remarked how the tale sounded more like Mark Twain's humorous style than London's style. It was fun to hear Adam giggle as I read it.

Please give Jim my best for the holiday. Merry Christmas, 1998. And here is to our friendship of eleven years times three!

Love,

Hank

1999 Indiana University Press published Nuwer's "Wrongs of Passage."

Nuwer and his work and website were featured in an A & E documentary on hazing.

Nuwer awarded Distinguished Alumni Award from Buffalo State. He established the Hank Nuwer Collection at Butler Library in honor of Fraser Drew and Joe Nikiel, donating signed letters and books and his manuscripts as his gift to the College.

Part V

Hazing As a Social Issue

(1999-2001)

108. Nuwer to Drew
Anderson, Indiana
January 8, 1999

Dear Professor Bob:

Happy New Year. I'm writing as a ferocious blizzard rat-a-tats my sixth-floor office window. I need to get home soon, lest I get stuck to the hubcaps, so this will not be a long letter.

Anyway, I wanted to write for a number of reasons. Adam was enthralled with you and your home. He seldom is in awe, but he was when he talked about your view and ["the pagan-killing hot tub." Jenine and I loved the visit. You looked spry enough to lead us on a charge to the nearest pub— or a trip to Barnes & Noble to have a cup of cocoa. Maybe next visit.

I'll drop a few things in this envelope. Mostly what I hope you'll find pleasurable in this envelope is the picture of son Christian and his "faire" Susan, married last August 15. Thank you for the gift you sent them. I understand they sent you a thank you.

You also will find my syllabus for this semester's journalism class at Anderson University and one for a special topics course I teach in the fall for the Indiana University School of Journalism at IUPUI. You'll see from the reading assignments why I love to keep at least a toe dangling in Lake Academe.

You may be confused at first why I am dropping the John Unterecker pages from Columbia University in this envelope. Well, you and I had talked last visit about how we both had written to Unterecker, the biographer of Hart Crane. Lo & behold, Nuwer is in box six of Mr. U's correspondence. Professor Fraser Drew is in box nine.

Columbia should have put all of Unterecker's correspondence into a single box. Alphabetically, I would have been right after Anais Nin. I could have been one of the many men she was VERY close to. Forgive my blarney.

Here is a bit of well wishing for you, written with acknowledgment of its thievery from E. A. Robinson: "May no stranger ever shut a door that a friend opened long ago."

Love,

Hank

109. Drew to Nuwer
Buffalo, New York
25 January 1999

Dear Hank,

Yesterday I updated the Nuwer section of Volume II of my illustrated autobiography by adding several pictures sent by you and Jenine—you three on the shores of [Lake] Superior, Jenine and father, Chris and Susan, you and Adam—so many good-looking people.

I may not write much tonight, as a couple of long incoming calls have slowed my progress at the very start. I want to enclose my Hemingway article which appeared in yesterday's Sunday [Buffalo] *News*. My presentation of his generous, kind, modest side is good contrast to the other writer's [Ed. Pulitzer-Prize winning John Balzar of the Los Angeles *Times*] characterization of him as boor, bigot and macho pig!

I fared well with the editors who spelled my name correctly, attributed me to BSC and not the University of Buffalo, and did only small violences. The plane [carrying Hemingway] that caught fire was a Rapide, not Papide—typographical [error]...The two paragraphs the *News* omitted I did not miss on first reading, and so I guess that was good editing.

I'll sign with love to all.

Bob

PS. My 90-year-old high school Latin teacher (she graduated from UVM at 19 and came to Randolph for her first teaching job when I was a senior) writes that she stood on the Great wall of China last summer. What a lady! She traveled with grandchildren to the Orient*.

Ed. Her name is Muriel Chatterton.

110. Nuwer to Drew
Anderson, Indiana
March 25, 1999

Dear Professor Bob:

You sure have a great fan in son Adam. When your postcard came he called out excitedly to his friend that you were the "cool professor" he had told him about.

My next book on hazing *Wrongs of Passage* comes out in September. Although it's premature, I'm sending along the dedication. It is a small repayment for all your support over the years.

Oh, and this quotation from Robinson Jeffers starts the next book— perfect for a book on hazing: "The cold passion for truth hunts in no pack."

Thank you for submitting the Buffalo State College Distinguished Alumnus Award. I am grateful, although I suspect writers are more likely to be considered for Distinguished Reprobate—and well deserved, too. Here, here!

I really never expected to get it and was floored to hear from Kate Ward of the alumni office with the news. Your direction and encouragement over thirty-five years have been the main reason I'm still trying so hard to achieve today. Your generous spirit always has moved me.

I wrote Kate a bit of what I was trying to do careerwise over the years and how your influence put me back on track whenever I looked ready to derail.

Love,

Hank

101 Portside, Buffalo, NY 14202
12 June 2000

STATE UNIVERSITY COLLEGE AT BUFFALO
1300 ELMWOOD AVENUE   BUFFALO, NEW YORK 14222

Dear Hank, Tenine and Adam,
    Last night I watched the NBA Game
No. 3. I had hoped that the Pacers would win because they had lost
the first two games and I am not an admirer of Shaq and I knew
they were your team. But early in the game I became quite fiercely
partisan and was delighted that Indiana won. I had not seen them
play before because I've never been a follower of pro basketball, but
now I am a Reggie Miller fan and I like Jalen Rose, the big baby-
faced Smit and Austin Croshere. I think the latter played for
Providence College and once gave me fits in a game against Duke.*
I'll be watching Game No. 4. Shaq of the Lakers used to annoy me
when he played for LSU.   I remember all the 1991 ballyhoo for
Shaq when LSU came up to Cameron. He got 9 shots, scoring 15 points
while Laettner had 24 points and Duke won 88-70. Next-year Duke
went down to LSU and Shaq was going to get even. He scored 12 points
to Laettner's 22 and Duke won again 77-67, Laettner getting 12 of his
points late in the second half with a young Grant Hill making some
contributions. I had to look up the exact numbers in my yearbooks
but the main facts I well remembered.
       Jim phoned this morning from cruise
ship on the River Neva about to dock at St. Petersburg. He and Nuts
are having two good weeks in Russia. Yesterday my old early Buffalo
roommate called from Connecticut – they are 80 and 83 and very
conservative Republicans. They have a pet quail who lives in the house
and will sing on the phone if prompted. His name, of cruise, is Dan.
He always sings for me although he must have been told that
I am a liberal Democrat. Maybe he knows that I have Indiana friends.
       I'm sure that you followed the French
Open, Tenine. I had hoped Monica Seles might come all the way back
and she fought hard in the quarterfinal, but Mary Pierce deserved
a win at the French after many tries. I like Guga Quenten who
won the men's title for 2nd time and I was pleased to see in the stands
my old favorite Ga...

111. Drew to Nuwer
Buffalo, New York
23 April 1999

Dear Hank,

A gorgeous, panoramic sunset here after a solid week of rain.

I seem to be recovering some of the vitality lost to the three-months cold but still have a sinus involvement, which leads me to honk like a demented goose (gander). I keep the windows shut tight lest one of the Canadians flying overhead hear me, misinterpret my meaning, break formation and land on my terrace expecting a warm welcome. "Leda and the Swan" made a lasting impression on me early in life: poultry are not to be taken lightly.

Your envelope here. The list of [signed] books and letters and other literary property going to Buffalo State's Butler Library is very impressive—very interesting items and very big names. This is a valuable as well as useful collection and I hope it will be appreciated. I used to know [archivist] Mary Karen Delmont fairly well when I was on campus, as well as her predecessor Sister Martin Joseph. You probably know that my Langston Hughes letters and first editions are at BSC, given in memory of Dean Ralph Horn of the Rockwell-Rice eras, and there are some signed Masefields there in memory of Dr. Rockwell and others. Would you mind if I told Mary Karen what a fine collection I think it is? *...It is a very fine gift.*

Commencement is not too far away. I look forward to seeing you all and to attending my first commencement in a long, long time. I stopped going in the Johnstone era because the rites seemed to have lost all dignity and because the floor-length heavy faille robe and regalia of mine was becoming a real burden to bear. I assume you will be in civilian attire. We emeriti, I believe, may go in full panoply and march with the faculty or go in ordinary clothes and sit with the great, unmasked public. I'm for the latter.*

Seriously, it will be good to be there and to see you all.

Love,

Bob

Ed. Drew sat in the BSC bleachers with his namesake Adam Robert Drew Nuwer, Nuwer's mother Theresa and then-wife Jenine.

112. Nuwer to Drew
Anderson, Indiana
May 18, 1999

Dear Professor Bob:

Saturday was a day for thrills [BSC Distinguished Alumnus], but mainly I wanted to thank you for your wonderful company through the day. My mother loved your home [on the Buffalo waterfront with its enormous plate glass window]. "This is my kinda livin' though I never made it," she said. She's so funny and direct. Adam was so pleased to see you again, as was Jenine.

The honor itself was a tremendous thrill for me. I also loved meeting President Muriel A. Moore* and administrator Tom Kinsey and all the library Special Collections people such as Maryruth Glogowski and Mary Delmont.

Well, it's a hectic day, and I have an adjunct computer-assisted reporting class at Anderson University to teach in thirty minutes. But deep down I still feel the glow from Saturday and thank you for nominating me.

RE: The Fraser Drew-Joe Nikiel Collection. If the library ever does an exhibit [as Drew had suggested to Delmont) of materials, perhaps you and I can see it together. It was an honor to name the collection for you and Joe Nikiel.

Love,

Hank

Ed. Later to known by her married name, Howard.

113. Drew to Nuwer
Buffalo, New York
20 June 1999

Dear Hank:

It is a beautiful Father's Day here, far above Niagara's waters. I never dreamed I would be father to a three-year-old Chihuahua at my age. It's good, Hank, that you have Adam there to celebrate the day and that you saw Christian not long ago. He and Susan are a fine-looking pair.

Jim is in town for a week, including my 86th birthday, and Mutsuo flew in yesterday for a few days. The beautiful birthday card shines on my desk, and I have been enjoying the various enclosures. I was surprised by your Internet contact with David Throne and his references to the Old Mentor. I've been neglecting Dave of late and so wrote to him. He lives in Littleton, Colorado.

I will remind you of my first meeting with Dave. One hot summer session he arrived on opening day wearing only the absolute legal minimum plus dark glasses and a mane of blond hair. I gave him minimal attention to which he responded courteously. On the first hour test he scored the highest grade in class. At the end of post-mortem class he lingered until all others had gone and came to the desk and said quietly, "Fooled you, didn't I?"

He took two graduate courses later, wearing more clothes and less hair but still getting the A grades. He has kept in touch over the years, often by phone, and he's been in Colorado now at least a decade.

Indiana University Press issued a handsome catalog and did well, I thought, with your *Wrongs of Passage*. The day of publication draws night and I wish great reviews and reactions from important quarters.

Love to all,

Bob

114. Nuwer to Drew
Anderson, Indiana
November 15, 1999

Dear Professor Bob:

So very sorry to hear that you have had strong discomfort with your eyes. I hope that has been cleared by the operation? Are you prepared for another Buffalo winter? Tell me if you need anything sent your way.

I have another long interview coming out in a new book for the University of Florida Press. It is called *Getting Naked with Harry Crews* and is edited by Erik Bledsoe. Attached is my long essay on fraternity hazing for *Nuvo Newsweekly*. You are in the essay's conclusion.

I am also sending a copy of my new book *Wrongs of Passage*. Due to its scholarly tone and subject matter, it is having a hard time getting into bookstores but is selling very well online through Amazon.com. I'll have a piece from *Wrongs of Passage* published as a commentary in the *Chronicle of Higher Education* in a week or two. I think our old *Courier* friend Mitch Gerber, now at the *Chronicle*, may be a copy editor on it, but I'm not sure.

I donated more stuff to Buffalo State Library for the Fraser Drew-Joe Nikiel collection—letters by Thom Gunn and William Least Heat Moon, a *Wrongs of Passage* draft, etc.

I am helping three graduate students with their doctoral dissertations on hazing or like topics, three M.A. thesis writers, and Lord knows how many undergraduates doing term papers. I lost track of all the doctoral dissertations I have been in for my interviews with authors or the hazing work. Maybe it is the next best thing to writing a dissertation myself—smile.

Adam has shot up in height—suddenly. He is as tall as Jenine. That pleases your namesake as you can imagine. He is such a great kid.

Love,

Hank

2000 Scholastic published Nuwer's book *High School Hazing.*

115. Drew to Nuwer
Buffalo, New York
11 April 2000

Dear Hank,

Today I saw on CBS the hazing in sports program *Rites & Wrongs*. I missed the very beginning but was thinking "How can they do anything on hazing without Hank?" when—there you were, looking mature and sage but still my boy. Then after sociologist Lionel Tiger, there you were again. This, of course, pleased me very much.

It was good to hear that you had taken an evening off to see a Martin McDonagh play, *The Beauty Queen of Leenane*. That "British" playwright isn't cheerful but he's good, I think.

I haven't had the energy to go out even to a McDonagh play. I'm going to attempt the memorial service for Paul Bulger at the college Saturday, riding there with Edna Lindemann, director emerita of the BSC Burchfield-Penney Art Center.

Jim went to New York City for two weeks, leaving me well provisioned. Today we have snow again—*ochone!*—an Irish exclamation of lament. I laid my bones in front of the fireplace for two generous naps today, both two-dog naps. The sweet-faced Chihuahua snores like a Great Dane.

Sent Adam a birthday note with a bill (not check) in it.

Love,

Bob

116. Drew to Nuwer
Buffalo, New York
17 April 2000

Dear Hank:

Thank you for *High School Hazing* [published by Scholastic] which should be a useful book. The many pictures should add to its impact and appeal, too. I hope that schools and young people will buy it.

At the reception in the Burchfield Art Center yesterday after the memorial service for Paul Bulger, Bob Stephen, a Bulger disciple and BSC administrator, said he had been in college with you and was happy for your success.

Tom Fontana, Tom Calderone, Tom Shannon and Julia Piquette were inducted into BSC's Communication Department Hall of Fame Saturday night. Julia was in absentia because she had plane, hotel, ballet, opera, theatre reservations in New York City of long standing.

I'm still weary on Monday and neck is stiff from the large number of alumnae ladies of the Bulger era who fell upon it Saturday afternoon.

Love,

Bob

117. Nuwer to Drew
Indianapolis, Indiana
September 21, 2000

Dear Professor Bob:

First, a happy birthday, belated to Jim. Then greetings to you. How is your health?

It has been a busy month or five weeks. I have had interviews with ABC News, *New York Times*, an A & E special on hazing, and must do three TV show appearances next week. Also I have lectures at University of North Carolina-Wilmington, Chico State in California and Auburn next week. Book sales are flat, however.

The sad news is that son Chris's grandmother, Alice's mother, passed away after a brutal bout with cancer and long-term diabetes. She loved good puns and bad puns, tiny dogs, her grandchildren, and sitting around a table with good talk and percolating coffee. She went on Chris's birthday, the fifteenth of September. I wish it were not so for him and her.

Chris was expecting the death but it was still rough, his first loss on his mother's side. He was eleven when my father, his grandfather, passed away.

I see that critics have roasted Jay Parini for his Robert Frost biography. I am reading a biography of Mary McCarthy, *Seeing Mary Plain*, by Frances Kiernan. The format is odd. Biographer Kiernan puts in lots of direct quotations to break up her text. I hate the technique. It [Irritation] prevents me from reading much at a stretch. I'm also reading Mary McCarthy's *The Groves of Academe*. She slightly reminds me of Jane Smiley, author of *Moo* as a satirist. Has anyone written a pleasant look at academe in fiction, hmm?

My birthday was good, made better by your welcome note. I heard from Buffalo State College archives. They have been working on the "Fraser Drew-Joe Nikiel Collection." Welcome news. The director Maryruth Glogowski caught me on ABC-TV News and wrote.

Love,

Hank

118. Nuwer to Drew
Indianapolis, Indiana
18 October 2000

Dear Prof Bob:

I am sending this sad and shocking news from the Oct. 4 issue of the Chico State *Orion* (California). Perhaps needless to say, I've been hit with the first prolonged bout of sleeplessness that has hit me since the soul-troubling divorce and after-divorce period of 1976-1977, and the awful miscarriage and the death of Dad in 1984.

In cold print, my words next to the story about Adrian Heideman's hazing death so near to my visit to Chico remind me of the character giving the warning to the departing *Pequod* crew in *Moby-Dick*. This was especially sad because I rarely form friendships at these ephemeral speech gatherings, but this time I formed a friendship with one older and one younger administrator at Chico. We went out to breakfast, shared an interest in tropical fish, reading and fishing, etc. I have been in touch with him since. A younger adviser, who invited me, is equally devastated. "A death was something I tried to prevent," he told me on the phone to break the sad news of Adrian's death.

Adrian spoke fluent Japanese, was an exchange student to Japan in high school, and recently played the drunk in *Les Miserables* in a Palo Alto, California community play. The irony of that role he played would make anyone sob.

I'm gathering back my composure and must do so quickly. I have talks at the University of Michigan, Central Michigan and several other schools and libraries coming up, and then I will take a break from speaking about hazing because it is too wrenching. I'm also speaking to high school students in the Episcopal diocese of Arlington, VA. The press has usually been kind to me, and I now am doing about two interviews a day. *The New York Times* called last night again, and I was immersed in *Chronicle of Higher Education* coverage of the $6 million hazing settlement for Scott Krueger, the unfortunate Orchard Park lad who died in a hazing at M.I.T.

My adjunct journalism class at IUPUI goes well, but students today skip an awfully large amount of classes, and I seem to get suckered more often than not into helping them make up the work.

I was sorry to read about the rocky trail of maladies that you have to tred upon these days, but glad to hear that you may visit the BSC President. Give a wave to a certain recessed office in Ketchum Hall where perhaps in some other time dimension the ghosts of wise Drew and lesson-needy Nuwer were bent over opposite sides of the great wooden desk with Celtic memorabilia distracting the student from time to time.

A pile of papers to grade, an *Indianapolis Monthly* assignment on the perils of coal ash, and other letters give me a bugle call to halt now.

Thank you for sending your memoir "Summer Dream of the Blasket." It made an afternoon in Indiana memorable for this reader, and I thank you for the thoughtfulness in making exquisite Gladys Gleason Brooks a memorable person in my own life.

Love from your student, Jenine and Adam.

Hank

2001 Indiana University Press published an updated volume of Nuwer's *Wrongs of Passage*.

119. Drew to Nuwer
Buffalo, New York
6 August 2001 and 8 August 2001 (same letter)

Dear Hank.

Today is the birthday of Mrs. F. D. Carpenter, the never-folding lady whom you quoted in the *Arts Indiana* piece.* She was the ultimate faculty wife, spouse to the head of the German Department at the University of Vermont and good friend of my friend Gladys Gleason Brooks. She fed this hungry and often penniless undergraduate many a meal and once gave me a ring worn by her father, Rhode Island Supreme Court Associate Justice John Taggart Blodgett, 1859-1912. Several years ago, scenting mortality, I sent it to the second of the three sons and had a fine, reminiscent letter from him. And from thoughts of Gwen Carpenter I turn to you.

I was glad, as always, to hear from you and I read the reviews of *Wrongs of Passage* with keen interest. I'm happy that you'll be doing a videoconference at the University of Vermont this fall. Connell Gallagher of Bailey/Howe Library is a good correspondent, is from County Donegal, Ireland people, and is a Robinson Jeffers enthusiast. If you have time for a salute, look at the Boulder in front of the Old Mill [residence hall], the university's oldest edifice. It is the university's special symbol and on 2 May 1932 I stood beside it with four other rising senior men to be inducted into Boulder Society by President Guy W. Bailey with a full ROTC military review—one of five peaks of my undergraduate life and perhaps the highest.

Today's mail brought a good letter from an early 1960s vintage UVM fraternity brother, an Owl named Woody Widlund. I once sent him a copy of your *Arts Indiana* piece, and he wrote back of his Robert Frost memories. His father had managed the beautiful Old Middlebury Inn when Frost was often at his Ripton farmhouse and the Bread Loaf Writers' Conference, and he would sometimes drive Frost home after a long night in the Inn bar, often with literary contemporaries.

Love, Bob

Ed. Drew had written "Do Not Bend or Fold" on a packet he mailed Mrs. Carpenter. She wrote back that "Mrs. F. D. Carpenter admits that on occasion she might bend but will never fold."

120. Nuwer to Drew
Indianapolis, Indiana
October 1, 2001

Dear Professor Bob:

I had good luck on 9/11 when I was supposed to be in New York City for a TV show taping. I dawdled thanks to an interview on hazing I did for my next book [*The Hazing Reader*] outside the city that didn't finish until 2 a.m. I never made it into the city because the bus line stopped cold after the first plane hit the World Trade Center. Horrible—or "The Horror," as Joseph Conrad wrote.

My other trip to the University of Vermont to tape a videoconference on hazing went well, as did a recent trip to Canton, New York, to speak.

Otherwise, busily engaged on Vonnegut research.

Hope that all is great.

Love,

Hank

Part VI

The Retiree and the Mature Writer

(2002-2008)

121. Nuwer to Drew
Haiku, Hawaii
April 26, 2002

Hello Professor Bob, or should I say Aloha:

Greetings from Maui. Any town named Haiku is a great town, indeed. My traveling companion as I camp in a tent by the ocean is William Dean Howells' *A Modern Instance* with an introduction by an Indiana-Duke University emeritus professor Edwin H. Cady.

Love,

Hank

2002 Nuwer was employed by Franklin College in Franklin, Indiana, as an assistant professor.

Scholastic published Nuwer's *To the Young Writer*. The New York Public Library named it one of the best juvenile books of the year by. Among others chapters included interviews with multicultural author Toyomi Igus, sportswriter Dale Ratermann, young adult novelist Phyllis Reynolds Naylor, journalist Patrick O'Driscoll and children's writer Rebecca Kai Dotlich.

122. Drew to Nuwer
Buffalo, New York
27 July, 2002

Dear Hank:

I liked your remembering your grandparents in your last letter.

Amelia Drew and Victor Fraser died before I was born. But I remember George Washington Drew the village blacksmith and Kate Fraser, famous for her angel cakes. My grandfather, the blacksmith, chewed tobacco which posed a menace to young boys seated in the back of his Model T Ford touring car.

This morning your new book *To the Young Writer* [Scholastic] came and delighted me, even if I have been able to read thus far only your preface and the Rebecca Dotlich and Max Aguilera-Hellweg sections—all fine.

Love,

Bob

123. Nuwer to Drew
Indianapolis, Indiana
August 1, 2002

Dear Professor Bob:

The dateline on this letter is Indianapolis, but I'm leaving soon for Oxford, Ohio, to address *pro bono* a conference of Phi Delta Theta this weekend. I love Oxford, its Old Main building and the streets of stone still in place, and its memorial to civil rights activists who assembled here to go to Mississippi. Not all returned. From Oxford I travel to Indiana University in Bloomington to present on athletic hazing.

I am glad your eyes are returning to reading shape. Thank you for taking a look at *To the Young Writer*. I liked Angelo Pizzo very much— self-effacing, humble, wise and helpful.

My own reading of late is *Truman* by David McCullough, Robert Putnam's *Bowling Alone*, and the best first novel I have read in years, *The Russian Debutante's Handbook* by Gary Shteyngart. Read the latter with a Kleenex box near you to mop tears of laughter.

Love,

Hank

124. Drew to Nuwer
Buffalo, New York
10 August 2002

Tomorrow Jim will be 73. I remember him when he was 22 and a student in one of my classes. He sat in back row and said nothing unless questioned, was shy and polite. When he was 29 and doing some graduate work he spoke to me in the BSC cafeteria and gave me a ride home. The long partnership developed from that.

It has been a big summer for BSC alumni back in touch. In the early Fifties I had a bright guy named Nicholas P. (Nick) LaGattuta in both a graduate class and undergraduate classes. He later became a dean at SUNY Geneso. He called me a couple days ago and was astonished that I remembered his middle initial, his pretty wife Marianne and his black standard poodle named Pierre. We had a great visit by phone and may get together when he and Marianne return from a visit in the fall to Ireland.

Did I ever thank you for the catalog from the New York Public Library's Berg Collection? That is a keeper. I've spent a lot of time at this place and have seen several shows from the Berg (with whom I had some correspondence about their run of letters from John Masefield to publisher Grant Richards, who was also A. E. Housman's publisher and friend. I have a couple of good Masefield letters which interrupt that run. Thanks for a great catalog.

Happy birthday in advance.

Love to all,

Bob

125. Drew to Nuwer
Williamsville, New York
7 October 2002

Dear Hank,

Moving, as you know, can cut the contents of files, shelves and drawers and revise and update habits and records. My books are in fair shape but I go on to other matters, including an updated will.

My will is not complicated. Jim is executor, as I am his, but I may need a new contingent executor (should we both be eliminated by a big truck). The present incumbent is a nice lawyer but semi-retired.

I wonder if you would consider serving in this capacity should the need arise. It isn't likely to arise because Jim is seventeen years my junior and in good shape. If it should arise, your job would not be difficult. Do let me know one way or the other when you can.

Beware of Oktoberfests.

Love to all,

Bob

126. Nuwer to Drew
Franklin College
October 15, 2002

Dear Professor Bob,

Occasionally I get bad ideas. A few days ago I played in the Franklin College annual faculty-student flag football game. Now, I am not averse to coasting if either side were 68 points ahead. But we were tied all the way to the last seconds, and so pride outstripped reason. I played nearly the whole game as tackle on offense and defense.

Need I mention that the behemoth I guarded had the unfortunate moniker of Bubba and outweighed me by fifty pounds? Somewhere the followers of some Strange-God-Before-Me have issued a sage warning never to sacrifice one's torso to anyone named Bubba, but I missed the message.

And we *were* tied.

After we lost by two points I saw that my body looked as if Klee had handpainted my body in Assyrian purple and gold bruises. Enough, I can still walk—sort of—and the blood pressure is ok at 110 over 71.

I was so happy to see your new house. It was great to see you, the familiar framed pictures, the books. The visit with my mother went well. I wanted to eat at Polish Villa, but she wanted Boston chicken, and so my craving for pierogi will have to wait.

On to your good note. Yes, it would be an honor to serve as contingent executor. You know I am hopeful that you and Jim make it to cantankerous centenarian status, but I am a practical being as well as a sentimental one—so absolutely, your wish is my wish. Let me know anything I need to know.

I am reading some prose sketches by Henry Miller. His critical essay on Walt Whitman is brilliant. He makes the case that Whitman's vision was that of a sort-of happy anarchist. His analysis of several Whitman poems bestirred me, and I will reread Whitman again and one of the three Whitman biographies I own. Miller also alludes to Jeffers' *Women of Point Sur*. It is time I revisit that beloved book. I had forgotten Miller knew Jeffers. He calls him that somber genius. It has been 27 years since I visited Tor House. 27 years?—how can that be?

Well, I have papers to grade before I sleep, and papers to grade before I sleep.

Love,

Hank

2003 Nuwer traveled to Dresden, Germany to begin research on a Kurt Vonnegut scholarly biography for Indiana University Press.

Indiana University Press published Nuwer's *The Hazing Reader*.

Nuwer discussed hazing in high school, college and in gangs with Anderson Cooper on CNN.

127. Drew to Nuwer
Williamsville, New York
1 January 2003

Dear Hank,

I had planned to write or call you before you went to Dresden, but a head cold left me with no voice for the phone and no energy for writing or typing. And now you are in Germany. It would probably have pleased your father to know you were there. I hope you have a safe, pleasant, useful trip and accomplish all you wish to do.

Fred Shilstone's book on Byron (*Byron and the Myth of Tradition*) you sent is here, and I thank you for it. I'm reading minimally but have been able to get a few quick looks at Byron. I'm eager to get into it seriously.

Although my major interest as teacher, writer and collector has been in the first half of the Twentieth Century, the early Nineteenth Century poet Byron has always fascinated me with the romantic *Childe Harold*, the satirical *Don Juan*, the letters and his brief but spectacular life. Meetings of my University of Vermont fraternity, Lambda Iota, founded in 1836 when Byron had been dead only twelve years and was a literary, social and political hero of international reputation, always began with readings from a large *Complete Works of Byron* on the presidential desk.

My collection of Byron is neither extensive or unusual, but among the biographies and editions of letters and poems is an interesting group of autographs. Its centerpiece is a letter in Byron's bold and unmistakable hand written at 8 St. James's Street in London on 6 June 1809 and addressed to his old manservant Joe Murray back at Newstead Abbey, the Byron ancestral home. "Mr. Murray," it reads, "The minute you receive this you will set off for London in some of the coaches with Robert [Rushton] and take care that he conducts himself properly. Be quick. Byron."

On 2 July Byron set out for the Mediterranean on his first European visit, accompanied initially by Joe Murray, Robert Rushton, a farmer's son who would serve as page, the valet [William] Fletcher [who was with the poet 1808 until Byron's death], a German servant Friese and Byron' lifelong friend, John Cam Hobhouse [a member of Parliament as Lord Broughton and Byron's best man at Byron's wedding]. The letter to Murray I secured with a statement of authenticity from Meyers of London in the early 1950's, along with several satellite documents from various British and American bookshops.

I may just ship this along in advance of your expected return from Dresden. I see you next plan January 2004 in London? Great. I think you will love London. My enthusiasm in 1964 was tempered by our week there coming at the end of a 68-day trek through Ireland, Scotland and England—and by a heat wave.

Love to all,

Bob

128. Nuwer to Drew
Dresden, Germany
January 6, 2003

Hello Professor Bob—*Glücklich Neujahr!*

Greetings from Dresden. It has been an exciting trip. I have been in the archives researching *Slaughterhouse-Five* and Vonnegut's prisoner of war experience. Yesterday I visited very near the slaughterhouse where he was a POW in 1945. Today I visited the hunting palace of Augustus the Strong and a thirteen-century cathedral in Meissen.

Love,

Hank

129. Nuwer to Drew
Dresden, Germany
January 7, 2003

Herr Bob—wie geht's?

Greetings from Eastern Germany, a few kilometers from the western Poland border of my mother's family.

I've exhausted my German, though enough comes back to order in restaurants, bookstores, my hotel, tourist spots. It is fun to be in bookstores and to understand German book titles.

Dresden is amazing. In some parts of the city I feel from the debris and ruined buildings that I am in Dresden three weeks after the 1945 bombing by allies. In some places in the city I feel I must be in modern Berlin—graffiti, blaring punk music, challenging teens. In some places where the Russians in the Sixties controlled East Germany, there are university dorms with tinted green windows, crumbly brick edifices, and so on.

One street is named after Martin Luther, another after Goethe. In the archives I learned two streets formerly were Adolf Hitler and Goering streets.

Wish me luck. I am trying to find Kurt Vonnegut's picture when he was issued POW dogtags. The records are incomplete in the last months of war, perhaps destroyed in the 1945 fire and bombing.

Love,

Hank

130. Drew to Nuwer
Williamsville, New York
13 January 2003

Dear Hank.

Greetings to the one who has sent wonderful cards from Dresden. I send this on a Buffalo State postcard, the place of our first meeting and some triumphs. You were great to find time in Dresden to write and send things. In time I'll ask more about your trip.

Did you know Art Professor Julius (Joe) Hubler at BSC? He was one of the best people there and close to Steve Sherwin. Now he has died, at 83, yesterday. Alas. Welcome home.

Love to all,

Bob

131. Drew to Nuwer
Williamsville, New York
16 February 2003

Dear Hank,

Another frigid weekend here.

A phone call from Vermont reports my one surviving Drew first cousin near death at eighty-six but no pain. My mother is always in mind around Valentine's Day. She died 50 years ago on 13 February.

It was good to hear that you had been speaking in Colorado and having a good reunion with the O'Driscoll [Pat O'Drscoll]. The Irish like to use definite article before a name, though strictly it is used thus to identify the head of the clan in Celtic society. I see that the Indiana University Press is publishing your book *The Hazing Reader*. I'm proud of the dedication to be in such good company.

I am glad that you and I are there in the BSC library in our various capacities. I have happy recollections of exhibits there from my collections, especially Ernest Hemingway in the late 1950s. Librarian Frances Hepinstall was a good friend and liked having the exhibits, which usually opened with a nice little reception hosted by Fran, with readings by Conrad Schuck and me. It always had a catalog I had prepared, which Fran had duplicated for distribution. I also liked her successor Lenore Kemp, and the current librarian Maryruth Glogowski who seems to be able and very pleasant.

Mutsuo Tomita is here for a few days before a long trip to the Orient, not his native Japan, but Beijing, Shanghai, Hong Kong, Taipei and other spots which I have never found beckoning. I used to find Mutsuo's own island, Hokkaido, fairly seductive, along with Vladivostok, Ulan Bator, and Tashkent, but not enough to lure me there. I do wish I had seen Paris, Venice and Ushuaia at the Argentine tip. But I did go to the ancestral places and to Havana!

Keep well, all of you.

Love,

Bob

132. Drew to Nuwer family in Indiana
Williamsville, New York
21 February 2003

I received a letter from Maryruth Glogowski, a very gracious recognition of your gifts to the library in support of the Nikiel-Drew Collection you established. The original collection was a fine gift for the library and your alma mater—and a heartwarming recognition of two friends, one of whom is still here to voice his appreciation.

I have just sent a response to Maryruth, with whom I spoke after the 1999 commencement convocation at which you were honored and at which your mother, wife, son and old mentor were proudly present. I treasure your notes from that occasion. I reminisce a bit in the letter to Maryruth about the earlier days of Butler Library, long-time director Frances Hepinstall, the various exhibits from my collections, and so forth. I should have told her about meeting Fran and her sister in the Great Southern Hotel in Galway in 1971.

The eyes have allowed me to do some very enjoyable reading in the two new biographies of Byron, the one you sent me by your former colleague Fred Shilstone and the one by Fiona McCarthy, which Tim Denesha and Dave Crosby brought on their last visit. Both books have new material and are very different from each other and the many earlier biographies.

When a faculty and curriculum change at Green Mountain Junior College where I was teaching in the later 1930s, moved me from Latin and French into English literature, I found Byron, along with Chaucer, Shakespeare, Hardy and Housman, the most popular writer in our anthology textbook. Later at Buffalo State College I enjoyed teaching an elective ambitiously titled "Byron and His Age."

Love, Bob

Ed. Fred Shilstone was one of a number of talented professors who made Nuwer's year of teaching at Clemson University truly memorable. Shilstone taught British Romanticism, and he and Nuwer shared a deep love for fine horses and literature or journalism about superior racehorses. In particular, the two men loved to discuss the merits of the great racehorse Timely Writer that Nuwer had profiled for

Boston *magazine. Sadly, Shilstone would die suddenly on August 23, 2005, distressing not only his friends but a legion of adoring students present and past. In an Internet tribute to Shilstone, colleagues and students ended with a quotation from Lord Byron. "Old Man! 'Tis not so difficult to die!"*

133. Nuwer to Drew
Denali Park, Alaska
June 10, 2003

Dear Professor Bob:

Denali has been great for wildlife sightings. I saw a rare gyrfalcon, numerous Arctic birds, Dali sheep, caribou, moose, three grizzlies. Am writing from a remote cabin.

I hope your birthday is spent in fantastic health.

I'm soon off to Anchorage. Adam flies in and joins me in Alaska. We camp in another remote cabin on a glacier way north.

Happy 90th.

Love, Hank

134. Nuwer to Drew
Fairland, Indiana
July 6, 2003

Dear Professor Bob:

Unfortunately, this note is the saddest I've written you since my dad's death. Jenine and I separated. If worse come to worse we will divorce, but we are determined to hold together in solidarity as the parents of Adam. We both are attending to his needs. There is nothing you can do, but your wonderful letters help immensely as bright lamps in dark passages.

Enough of this. I hope many former students remembered you on your 90th.

Love, Hank

2003 Nuwer and his sons Chris and Adam shared a deep love in common for the state of Alaska. The writer traveled there frequently for research, salmon and trout fishing, and to interview champion Iditarod sled racers such as Bill Mackey and his father Dick Mackey. While Chris had spent one memorable summer camping and working in a salmon cannery plant, his brother Adam finally made it to Alaska to join his father who was there to profile famed female racer Libby Riddles.

Nuwer continued researching the life of Kurt Vonnegut for a biography expected to be finished by December 2009.

135. Drew to Nuwer
Williamsville, New York
13 July, 2003

Dear Hank,

I have just re-read your letter once more after leaving it alone for a day. I grieve for all three of you that this happened. Most comforting is the fact that you and Jenine are united in your determination to protect and assist Adam. Of course, I am too far away, geographically and otherwise, to diagnose or prescribe. I send you love and support

You have been much in mind over this weekend. The weekend now draws to a close with a dinner out, once my favorite activity, but no longer so. We are going to Sinatra's, a very good Italian restaurant, to celebrate Mutsuo's 14 July (Bastille Day!) birthday. He is 68. I think Italian is Jim's favorite cuisine whether Sicilian, Tuscan or Venetian.

It is Mutsuo's favorite after Japanese, and of course he approves only the Japanese restaurants of Japan and New York City. No, I do not really like "ethnic cuisines." I continue to prefer the New England food of my childhood. I was generally happy with the often maligned food in England, Scotland and Ireland in the Sixties and Seventies. However, I do not care for the Scottish national haggis or such Irish dishes as blood puddings, crubeens, etc. I suppose if I had to choose the food of one country it would be French or German, with exceptions.

I enclose a piece linking Cocteau and Hemingway. Connell Gallagher is interested in the provenance of my books and papers given to UVM and he will file this.

Jean Cocteau and Ernest Hemingway were contemporaries but not friends. Their paths may have crossed in the Paris in the 1920s when the young Hemingway was an emerging writer whose associates included John Dos Passos, F. Scott Fitzgerald, James Joyce, Archibald MacLeish, Joan Miro, Pablo Picasso, Ezra Pound and Gertrude Stein. For a time Hemingway worked for the *Transatlantic Review* and, in the absence of its editor Ford Madox Ford, edited the July and August 1924 issues. In the first of these he managed to insult the already successful Cocteau.

Cocteau, Hemingway wrote, "has a very good minor talent and a certain amount of intelligence," was "amusing in French and often instructive" and, though unable to read or write English, had translated Romeo and Juliet into French, using "some school book edition of Shakespeare."

After this dismissal of Cocteau, one wonders how the As Stable Publications of Englewood, New Jersey, was able to secure a Cocteau drawing for the cover illustration of its 1926 pamphlet, Hemingway's play *Today Is Friday*. Three hundred numbered copies were printed, of which my copy 197 was secured at the 1950 Bernheimer auction, housed in the usual Bernheimer pigskin case.

Today is Friday is a one-act play, a dialogue among three Roman soldiers and a Hebrew wineseller in a drinking-place at eleven o'clock the night after the Crucifixion. The Cocteau drawing on the cover of the pamphlet is a male nude with right leg raised and head tilted upward. It is signed "Jean" with a small heart and the words below, "L'impuissance à convaincre."

I wrote to Jean Cocteau asking for an autograph to place in my copy of *Today Is Friday*. He responded with a page on which he had written "Avec l'amitié de Jean Cocteau, St. Jean Cap deFerrat, Alpes Maritimes, Août 1950," and three sheets with ink drawings of typical Cocteau heads, each signed and dated. I framed the page with the greeting with letters of Alice B. Toklas and Archibald MacLeish, and it hangs with framed letters of Ernest and Mary Hemingway.* One signed drawing I placed in *Today Is Friday*.

I hope your small farmhouse at Fairland is a good place to work. I think there is a Fair Isle halfway between the Shetlands and the Orkneys.

The ninetieth birthday gala ended yesterday, I suspect, with a couple of errant greeting cards and the picnic lunch brought by Suzanne Marvin Flynn and Deborah O' Hagan Daly, who were in the first class I taught at Buffalo State. Over the years they have kept in touch through the complexities of their own busy lives—four children each, many grandchildren, widowhood, teaching careers, abundant travel (often together as they maintained their college friendship with each other and with Rita Lawler O'Brian, Babe Hurley O'Connor and other Alpha Sigma Alpha sorority sisters.

They brought a sumptuous picnic lunch, enough for a dozen rather than the six who were here—Jim, Mustuo, I and Julia Piquette, my good friend. They loved our house and Chihuahua and we had a good time.

No more now. I pray for the resolution of your great and frightening problem. You deserve a happy resolution.

Love,

Bob

Ed. Letters written to Drew personally from the Hemingways.

2004 Nuwer played a major role in the PBS hazing documentary, *Unless a Death Occurs*, which focused on the death of a student at Plattsburgh State.

Nuwer destroyed seven ribs in a rodeo bullriding accident, later writing a participatory journalism story on the disaster for two magazines. Before checking into a hospital for surgery, he flew to Washington to deliver a major keynote address to a U.S. Department of Education audience, then caught a shuttle to New York and was interviewed about hazing on the *Today Show* by Matt Lauer. He flew back, underwent surgery and missed only one day of classes. Nuwer's students and colleagues packed his hospital room with visits and funny get-well cards.

136. Nuwer to Drew

Fairland, Indiana
October 27, 2004

Professor Bob:

Quick postcard to let you know I've had a physical setback. Crushed seven ribs while rodeoing in Ohio. Was thrown hard from a Brahma bull while bullriding. Will send you the magazine article recounting the debacle.

Love,

Hank

137. Nuwer to Drew

Fairland, Indiana
November 18, 2004

Dear Professor Bob:

Thanks for your good letter of November 9 and not coming down too hard on me for riding undomesticated bovine stock. Sounds as if Jim is busy with seasonal activities. I'm cleaning out email files, paper files and old student papers today.

Recovery continues. Hardest part is that fluid still occupies my chest cavity, misplacing my lungs upward and depriving me of full oxygen intake. Still, I make all my classes, amazing the surgeon who says anyone else with seven cracked, splintered and demolished ribs would be in bed for four weeks. But even I can't make bone grow faster in spite of my determination to heal. It will be April before the ribs seal and begin to look like a repaired cathedral arch, but I have to recover enough to visit Alaska in January. I have my ticket and hotel in hand.

Perhaps I'll bring the rodeo video of my ride when I see you next— unless you hate horror movies. I apologize if the bull story made you worry. I guess I am just one of those males who needs an athletic challenge now and then. *Mea culpa, mea culpa, mea maxima* etc.

I was happy to see Boston win the World Series in spite of my New York affiliation by birth. I played with Boston Manager Terry Francona in 1981 with the Expos Triple A team when I did the piece for *Denver Magazine* and the Buffalo *Courier-Express*. He was a rookie then and terribly nice to me.

Stay warm and healthy. Hola to Jim. I'm reading a Hemingway biography on the Paris years and was pleased to hear you are rereading him. I do plan to teach *The Dangerous Summer* next year during my Hemingway seminar for Franklin College.

Love, Hank

2005 Nuwer traveled to England with Thelma Moore, his confidante for many years. They visited London theaters, art galleries and literary haunts.

Nuwer married Lizabeth Klein of New York. Nuwer met Liz through the husband of her cousin Margie Robinson Cleary. Margie and Hank had worked together in a Los Angeles daycare center in 1976.

Nuwer traveled to Switzerland to write a screenplay with old Reno and Los Angeles writing partner, documentary filmmaker Gian Carlo Bertelli.

138. Nuwer to Drew
Fairland, Indiana
May 22, 2005

Dear Professor Bob:

Thanks for your newsy note, but I'm sorry for these losses of friends and students.

I have been teaching and speaking outside the classroom (Dartmouth, University of North Dakota; Southern Illinois, Edwardsville). I'll be in Denver when you get this, speaking at another conference co-sponsored by Security on Campus. But the good news is that I will enjoy a three-day mini-vacation later in the week. I'll stay in a cabin in the Rockies and do some hiking.

Happy birthday, Professor Bob. How will you spend it? I sent two fine books to [the library at] Buffalo State (one on civil rights and one Civil War biography) in your honor. I received a nice note from a

University of Buffalo librarian named Kathleen Quinlivan who spoke gloriously of her classes with you in the 1970s. She read the old *Arts Indiana* article on you that I had put online.

I had one fine assignment a few weeks ago. I played in a televised 1860 vintage baseball game in Cooperstown sponsored by Ball State University electronic field trips. The manager of the other team was Ozzie Smith. I hit a triple and my teammates complained. "Sire, ye run as if a piano were on your back," one shouted. I would have made home had I not stopped at second to strap on an oxygen tank.

*On to Denve*r. [Lacks the ring of *On to Richmond*.]

Love,

Hank

139. Nuwer to Drew
Lugano, Switzerland*
July 6, 2005

Dear Professor Bob: I've titled this postcard "For Whom the Bull Tolls!"*

Headed to Milan by train to see LaScala. I love the Italian side of Switzerland. In a few days I explore Zurich.

Love,

Hank

*Ed. *Type of Correspondence: Oversized postcard with bull with bell around its neck*

140. Nuwer to Drew
Fairland, Indiana
22 July, 2005

Hello Professor Bob:

Well, the alarm is set for 4 a.m., and I'm off to New York City…for Vonnegut research and some serious museum searching.

Italy and Switzerland were wonderful…Highlight of La Scala [in Milan] was indeed the museum—Verdi, Caruso, and so many other great names. It was exciting that my writing partner [Gian Carlo Bertelli] had his librettos used here at La Scala.

Adam is disconsolate. His mentor, welding teacher Lonnie Scott, died after a three-year fight with pancreatic cancer. In spite of pain, he taught almost to the end. Adam is miserable, and we [Jenine and I] are also, although we knew it was inoperable.

My mother's health has deteriorated, but she is a bit better. I will get up there to Buffalo soon.

Love,

Hank

141. Drew to Nuwer
Williamsville, New York
July 24, 2005

Dear Hank:

I regret the unhappy news of Adam's mentor and the illness of your mother. I'm glad that she is recovering and wish her the very best. Tell Adam I am *very sorry* about Lonnie Scott.

Love,

Bob

142. Nuwer to Drew
Fairland, Indiana
August 6, 2005

Dear Professor Bob:

My news is that I met a wonderful woman named Liz Klein from New York City through her cousin, my friend Margie Robinson Cleary, who taught preschool with me in Los Angeles in 1976. She's spirited and fun and energetic and supportive of my work. I'll attach her photo taken this month in New York. I'll be out of the country in the Dominican Republic with her this month.

Love,

Hank

2006 Nuwer, wife Lizabeth, and Franklin College colleague Ray Begovich took students to Paris, France for a January excursion. They visited the Louvre, Hemingway's haunts, and many museums for Nuwer's "Hemingway Nonfiction and Journalism" course.

Buffalo State College awarded an honorary doctorate to Nuwer. In brief remarks at Commencement, Nuwer thanked Fraser Drew for his four decades of mentoring.

143. Drew to Nuwer

Williamsville, New York
13 January 2006

Dear Hank and Lizabeth,

Welcome home from France, the country I loved when a little boy during World War I. As you can see from this postcard of the Chapel of Newstead Abbey, I am using up a stack of cards brought home from the 1964 summer in England, Scotland and Ireland. We spent several days at Byron's ancestral Newstead Abbey, his burial church St. Mary Magdalene in Hucknall Torkard, and in his Gordon mother's native Scotland.*

I'm sure you had a memorable time in Paris on the Hemingway expedition and that the students saw, learned, heard and felt much. Thanks for keeping in touch as you prepared for the trip.

Love,

Bob

Ed. George Gordon Byron was the son of Catherine Gordon, heir of the Laird of Gight.

144. Nuwer to Drew
Fairland, Indiana*
January 20, 2006

Dear Professor Bob:

Liz and I safely have returned from Paris. We visited all the old Hemingway haunts and the former Sylvia Beach Shakespeare & Company bookstore. For good measure we threw in the Gertrude Stein salon, a Henry Miller haunt, Ezra Pound's old home, the Louvre (three times!), the Delacroix Museum and the Pablo Picasso Museum.

Love,

Hank and Liz

Ed. Note was sent on a postcard of Ernest Hemingway's domicile in Paris on Rue du Cardinal Lemoine.

145. Nuwer to Drew
Fairland, Indiana
January 24, 2006

Dear Professor Bob:

I just sent a box of books to Maryruth Glogowski in Buffalo State Special Collections in honor of your next birthday in June. How's that for anti-procrastination? I came back with some kind of Paris germ and am wheezing like a Jeep with a ruptured radiator.

Love, Hank

146. Drew to Nuwer
Williamsville, New York
25 January 2006*

Dear Hank,

This postcard was a place of pilgrimage in the summer of 1964. Housman's ashes lie just outside the church wall on the north side. Thanks for card of Hemingway and 74 rue de Cardinal Lemoine. I'm glad [your] Paris adventure was a good one with time for the visits to the Louvre and bows to Stein, Pound, Miller, Picasso and Delacroix. And Sylvia Beach, of course.

I was delighted by the phone message from you with the good news in the letter from Muriel Howard.

When one's students are awarded honorary doctorates, one may lie back on his chaise lounge and relax in satisfaction. I'd like to think that on that day in May I shall rise from my bed and move majestically down to 1300 Elmwood to attend the hooding or investiture…*Well deserved, mon fils.*

Love,

Bob

*Ed. Type of Correspondence: Handwritten postcard of Ludlow Parish Church, Shropshire, England

147. Drew to Nuwer
Williamsville, New York
6 February 2006

Dear Hank,

Philip Errington was here three hours between New York City planes on what was luckily one of my good days. He is the Number One Masefield man in this century and came from London to pay respects to an old Masefield dog.

We signed each other's books and Jim gave us a nice lunch and drove Philip back to the airport. He is also Sotheby's director of printed books and manuscripts and photographed the inscription pages of the best Hemingways. "If you ever decide to sell, we are the best."

Love,

P. Bob

148. Nuwer to Drew
Fairland, Indiana
April 1, 2006

Dear Professor Bob:

Happy April Fool's Day, St. Patty's Belated, and Easter—all bundled in one greeting.

It has been so hectic here working at two schools and freelancing. Grabbing a quiet moment to write you is a real treat for me. This is Spring Break at Franklin College, but my IUPUI class meets today. So it's a semester without a break, really, although I plan to snatch blocks of time to spend with Liz and Adam and my writing—and some reading time.

I'm writing just an hour a day, fighting to get Vonnegut and my kid's novel written.

I picked up a copy of *The Best Short Stories of 1923*. Does that ring a gong? Yes, it is the collection of short stories edited by Edward J. O'Brien that bears the dedication, misspelled, "To Ernest Hemenway" and the story "My Old Man," also by Mr. "Hemenway." As you probably remember, Hemingway's story was one of the ones that survived after his first wife Hadley lost the suitcase full of stories in 1922. I wonder if this O'Brien was trying to do a good deed for Hemingway in publishing a previously unpublished story. I see also in this collection the familiar names of contributors Sherwood Anderson, Theodore Dreiser and Irvin S. Cobb.

Liz and I did get away for an hour the other day to fish at a nearby lake, which is more a pond, really. She found herself with about a fifteen-pound catfish on a four-pound test line. After a battle resembling Santiago from *The Old Man and the Sea* and his heroic angling effort, she got the beast on the sandy shore, only to see the line break. And so, "Moby Meow," as this catfish shall ever be dubbed, wriggled and disappeared into the pond's murky denizens. Because the reel broke, I helped her pull it in by the line only. Liz said that wasn't fishing, it was "*flossing* a fish to shore."

We also went out on a Friday to dance at a country western place. We had fun trying to learn to line dance.

Adam celebrated his 21st birthday working at his job. We got him some airbrushing books and Monte Python tee shirts with sayings he likes.

I have ordered a huge batch of Indiana University Press books pre-selected and approved by Maryruth Glogowski for Butler Library. These will be in honor of your birthday.

Love, Hank

149. Drew to Nuwer
Williamsville, New York
10 May, 2006

Dear Hank, alias Dr. Nuwer,

This holiday card is not quite appropriate, although I hope that your visit to Western New York had holiday elements. I like the picture of you on the front page of *Buffalo State Insider*. I have cut it out to insert in the Nuwer section of Volume II of my autobiographical albums (text and pictures). I am so pleased about your gifts to the college library.

Ed Rosinski '50 was named Distinguished Alumnus. He has had a great career. I sent him a congratulatory note yesterday to San Francisco and told him I hoped that you and he had met over the weekend.

Two recent deaths. One was my favorite second cousin, Becky Cremer of Hilo and Sonora, California. She was Rebecca Ann Fraser of Woodstock, Vermont, member of U.S. Olympic Ski team in 1948, and almost a carbon copy of her great aunt, my mother. The other was the only child (Bob) of my colleague and friend Estella Schoenberg, a John Milton scholar and author of a book on William Faulkner, who came to Buffalo State about the time you graduated. Bob leaves his mother, a Russian wife and young son; he taught part-time at the college.

Yesterday I went out into the garden and watched the koi in the pond and waterfall. I even walked around a bit and feel a bit more like my vigorous younger self. Mostly I rest and paw over my albums, books and letters.

Love,

Bob

150. Nuwer to Drew
Fairland, Indiana
May 15, 2006

Hi Professor Bob:

Well, it's 4 a.m. with coffee already brewed and my hazing web page already loaded on the Internet with news stories. Northwestern University's women's soccer is imbedded in a hazing controversy. A high school boys' athletic team has allegations against the coach for sexual hazing on a team bus. These are not the kinds of hazing incidents I wrote about fifteen years ago. Either these things were kept undercover then or times have changed for the worse. The behaviors are disturbing. I speak Monday through Wednesday at the University of Colorado on the topic of student violence.

I really, really enjoyed Buffalo State Commencement and the numerous nice people I saw, including Maryruth.

I hope Buffalo State can get you a videotape of my acceptance speech for the honorary doctorate. It was impromptu. I had been reassured that no remarks were needed. But President Muriel Howard kindly and thoughtfully offered me the microphone.

I'm sorry you could not attend Commencement, but I was pleased to visit you and hear you have mustered strength to go into the garden. I can see you there now with a thin volume of poetry, eyes moving from koi in the pool to perhaps Andrew Marvell's "To His Coy Mistress" on the page. That's a happy scene.

The Buffalo State folks really made Lizabeth and me seem like family. Lizabeth made several friends at Buff State. We loved "Mickey,"

Muriel Howard's husband. He turned out to be like me, a devotee of the Isaac Walton sport and pastime. Did I ever tell you that the New York Public Library had ALL the Walton editions of the *Compleat Angler* the time I was at the library to accept an award for *To the Young Writer*? I was thrilled.

Time to bench press. Today is heavy lifting day on weights.

Love, Hank

151. Nuwer to Drew
Fairland, Indiana
May 30, 2006

Hola Professor Bob:

No, I'm not in Mexico but I am cooking Mexican chili now.

Liz and I were in Colorado last week. After I delivered two lectures on campus violence at the University of Colorado, we broke bread with old University of Nevada friend Patrick O'Driscoll, the *USA Today* reporter. He and Lizabeth shared stories and made a friendship. Then Liz and I made a beeline to Estes Park and the entrance to Rocky Mountain National Park.

I would love to send a note of appreciation to that inspiring Buffalo State teacher Eloise Courter. Her address? She loaned me a special book of hers on teaching that had her bookplate in it from St. Cloud State in Minnesota. She asked me to take special care of it because she valued that book, etc., etc. Can you see where this is headed?

Let me refresh your memory re the amount of goop and mud on the Buffalo State campus in the spring of 1968. The student union was under construction. I was bringing back her book.

Yep, I stepped out of my car in a parking place square in the mud and Dr. Courter's book pitched into the filthy water. I slunk into Ketchum Hall with that ruined copy between thumb and two fingers. She was so understanding. I was crushed and mortified. I think that episode may have cured me of checking out books from teachers and friends!

I am filing a mental image of you and Faun. What a great man-dog friendship you two have had. Speaking of canines, there is a very big coyote in the fields near Fairland. I hope you have a flurry of good days in your birthday month.

I'm leaving after eating for the airport for LaGuardia and New York, so forgive this rushed letter. I will be on ESPN with Stephen A. Smith.

Love,

Hank

152. Drew to Nuwer
Williamsville, New York
2 June 2006

Dear Hank:

Before it slips my mind, here is the address of Eloise Courter, who would be happy, I'm sure, to hear from you.

What a story that was about dropping Eloise's book in the Buffalo State mud. My heart ached for you forty years later, knowing your respect for teachers and for books. Eloise lives at a very nice retirement home where Julia Piquette of Buffalo State also lives. I have seen her there and once had dinner there when Jim, Mutsuo and I, along with Eloise, were Julia's guests. Eloise is indeed a fine person.

I loved the 2006 Buffalo State Commencement program and will keep it with an earlier one. I'm glad you inscribed it and I was proud to read my name in the description of you and your career. The importance of such recognition grows as one ages. As I read the program I came upon my name again in the roll of distinguished professors. The names brought back the past.

The college is quite different from the one I knew and watched change. I think Muriel is doing a great job. I'll bet that she and Mickey are fun off-campus. I'd find out if I were twenty, thirty, forty years younger.

Today I paid my monthly visit to Buffalo Medical Group Urology on nearby International Drive. There my favorite, the head urology nurse, plucked me out of the waiting room and changed my reservoir-and-aqueduct system with efficiency and speed, good humor, and a highly therapeutic hug or two, thus reducing physical discomfort and mental wear-and-tear.

The spring flowers have faded, but the iris are spectacular—blue, purple, black, white and a heavenly peach color. The pond lilies under the waterfall are lovely, and soon roses will be blooming. The scent of the lilacs takes me home to New England, and we have a slender laburnum, a gold chain tree, which takes me back to Tralee in Ireland. An enormous one in the Town Park there was destroyed in a thunderstorm between my fourth and fifth Irish visits.

I like your idea about the Nuwer-to-Drew letters and will have a look at the box in my closet and get back to you. I dislike adding such a chore to your schedule. If we do this, you are to take as much time as you need. I will see if I can put them in near chronological order.

Love,

Bob

154. Nuwer to Drew
Fairland, Indiana
June 6, 2006

I just walked to the post office to drop off your birthday card and a Buffalo State-bound crate of twenty-six books in honor of Fraser Drew. The latter is the start of the "Buffalo State Special Collections—Hazing" file of books, dissertations, films and articles. It is only a small start, but I mean to make it the single most distinguished educational collection devoted to hazing. Heck, for now it is the only one. So let us wave an orange-and-black pennant and give a silent cheer for our Buffalo State "We're Number One" status.

Your last letter was in the mailbox, and so I sit down twice today to write, this time at a less ungodly hour. Coffee number four sits before me somewhat reproaching me.

I liked what you wrote about Dr. Steve Sherwin. My one experience with him was outside the classroom. Somehow I fell one credit shy of graduating in June 1968. I met with him because I'd gotten a note from the English Department that said my graduation would be delayed until I could take another hour of gym in the summer. I was pretty crushed. But he gave me credit for playing baseball at Buff State and waived the credit. He was a nice, sensitive man.

I'm so glad the Drew Fan Club extends to the Buffalo Medical Group—Urology, and that they take such good care of you. Humor and hugs at Urology? Who knew?

Once, I went in for a urine test when I was young and was sent into the bathroom. The pretty nurse on duty said, "You'll find what you need in there." A few minutes later I came back out with about two-dozen test bottles in my arms. "It was a hard job, but I managed to fill them all," I said to the startled nurse. Before she could faint or have a fit I said, "just kidding," and went back into the bathroom to do my business in the solitary container. Ah youth!

Yes, President Muriel Howard is wonderful, and her husband Mickey is a hoot and smart and charming. Perhaps I can spirit him away one day to cast fishing lines before bass.

I have away trips for talks at Adelphi and Syracuse coming up. Hi to Jim. Liz sends blessings.

Love,

Hank

156. Drew to Nuwer
Williamsville, New York
9 August 2006

Dear *Famille* Nuwer,

After a couple days, dragging myself around, I have risen again to an occasion. On 6 August it was Dr. Nuwer and his lovely bride.

Today it is four ladies from the Buffalo classes of 1947 and 1948 who have been faithful friends of their dear old English professor for over half a century. The three widowed grandmothers from Buffalo State

'48 were sophomores in a literature class of my first semester—Sue Marvin Flynn, Debbie O'Hagan Daly and Rita Lawler O'Brian. The 4th of their Alpha Sigma Alpha group, Angela Hurley O'Conner, is not coming north from Savannah this year. She, by the way, has seven children—the three coming today have only 4 each. Today's fourth is Jean Moore Strong [Buffalo State]'47, whom I haven't seen in many years but with whom I keep in touch. They are due today at noon and we are serving lunch—sandwiches from Dash's which are attractive and delicious and a salad bowl and wine and coffee—to which Sue, a famous cook, is adding the dessert—a fresh peach pie. Jim likes them all.

Jim, who does not like everybody, is greatly taken with Madame Klein-Nuwer, whose smartly hyphenated professional name I found on her [business] card left with Jim. That makes two of us, three if one counts Hank (and I guess that one should). It was very good to see Hank after missing out on the Buffalo State commencement and to meet Lizabeth at last.

I'm happy about your new home and wish you many years of happiness in it.

In spite of the anniversary due on 19 August, Hank, you looked and acted like a 40-year-old. I hereby send congratulations a few days early although a card should turn up. I have been saving one from a wildlife organization with the legend "Happy Birthday, Tiger," but at the moment I seem to have misplaced it. I liked the sentiment.

The news involving son Christian and Susan with baby due in December was great. Does this make me an honorary great or great-great grandfather? I hope that Adam has a fine holiday in Nevada.

Fawn flourishes.

155. Drew to Hank
Williamsville, New York
19 August 2006

Dear Hank,

It is the morning of your sixtieth birthday, and in an hour or so I will try to reach you by phone.

I have already celebrated the day by playing the 2006 Commencement DVD, which arrived the day before yesterday from Muriel Howard's office. You looked very impressive and distinguished in full academic regalia, and I was proud of you.

Then you took the mike and graciously gave me the recognition, which few teachers are fortunate ever to receive. Not many of us, however deserving, are privileged to have a student like you who goes on to make a difference in this world and remembers a teacher who may have helped him along the way.

Thank you for remembering and for your enduring friendship.

Love,

Bob

156. Drew to Hank and Lizabeth Nuwer
Williamsville, New York
28 August 2006

Dear Hank and Liz,

I send two pictures from a recent visit to my study—we [Jim and I] have spoken often of your visit. We all keep busy in one way or another. I hope that your house plans move along well, and that you manage some writing time, Hank. We all keep busy in one way or another. I have been writing mini-memoirs of old friends of the University of Vermont, Duke, Green Mountain and Hartford days. It is amazing how bright and fresh the details of those days remain. I hope that my memory remains sharp even after the other faculties fade and diminish. Jim is preparing for his vacation in Venice. Mutsuo and I will endeavor to comfort Fawn during his absence. Good luck to you both.

Love,

Bob

157. Nuwer to Drew
Waldron, Indiana
November 8, 2006

Dear Professor Bob:

We have a "Newer Nuwer" at the house. It is a black Labrador retriever puppy. At first we called him Casey. However, because he has turned into a food thief, we changed his handle to Jesse James. It fits!

I bought a ticket for Alaska in January again. I will rough it some, but I also will work in the Alaska State Library on a long-term book project concerning a nineteenth-century hazing death that will begin when the Vonnegut biography gets finished at last.

Much love,

Hank

158. Nuwer to Drew
Waldron, Indiana
December 26, 2006

Dear Professor Bob:

Taking care of a sick black lab puppy today.

Wanted to wish you a hale and hearty New Year.

Hope you got my phone message that Zoey Noelle was a Christmas Eve baby born to son Christian and his wife Susan.

Sadly, my Aunt Blanche Lysiak Reis passed on Christmas Day. She was my godfather Mickey's wife. Her son Emil died young, and she has grieved ever since.

Now for the important question. How are you and Jim? Let us know if you need anything. Your Christmas gift to Buffalo State College Library "Fraser Drew Collection" is $1,000 from my next speaking engagement to Indiana corrections officials. This will bear your name.

I see that Dan DiLandro is working very hard to get the archives in shape. I see that the Drew gift of Langston Hughes poems is prominently mentioned.

I also see a newly added collection by someone I did not know, Dr David Lampe. Much looks medieval, but there is a good sprinkling of correspondence with contemporary poets, including Henry Taylor (remember that interview I did with the Virginian poet for *The South Carolina Review?*), and Ehrhardt, and Creeley.

Liz sends love, as do I.

Hank

2007 Nuwer was promoted to Franklin College associate professor and received tenure.

159. Drew to Nuwer
Williamsville, New York
19 January 2007

Dear Hank, Liz and Big Paws:

I'm not sure whether I have written to you since your visit or just dreamed that I wrote. My life, dreams, and the movies I watch seem to mingle these days as I continue to crumble.

Yesterday I did write, I'm sure, to Muriel Howard, wishing her and Mickey a happy New Year and mentioning your gift and visit and Connie Schuck's death in California.

Connie and wife Sammy go back to 1947 when I had been here only two years. Connie and I were playmates, you could say, for many years. I remember many lunches at The Place, The Quaker Bonnet and the Jafco Marina and going to Offerman Stadium, the Old Rock Pile, for Buffalo Bison baseball games. We used to give joint Readers' Theatre readings in the Union. I appeared on his TV show on Channel 4 and have the pictures to prove it, and he beat Bill Barnett, Gene Dakin and me in a 1949 Faculty Apollo contest arranged by the students. I never let him forget it. His wife Sammy, my favorite faculty wife along with Fran Sherwin, called and asked me to send a page about Connie to be read on a service on 27 January, and it went off to her yesterday, typed!

I hope that you are all three OK, and Zoey and family, and newly housed Adam. I wonder if you are finding any time (I don't see how), Hank, for editing the first box of Drew-Nuwer letters. I'm starting a new box. Good luck roughing it in Alaska.

Love to all,

Bob (and Jim)

160. Nuwer to Drew
Waldron, Indiana
January 24, 2007

Dear Professor Bob:

Was saddened to hear that your friend Connie Schuck passed. I enjoyed your memories of fun days going back to 1947, especially the Apollo nomination.

The Ithaca research trip to Cornell went very well. I also was filmed at Ithaca College in a documentary about hazing to be called *Haze: The Movie*. Robin Wright Penn will narrate the trailer online. Tomorrow I leave at 4:30 a.m. for Alaska via Minneapolis. I have a sleeping bag good to -30 degrees. I'll need it.

Love,

Hank

161. Drew to Nuwer

Williamsville, New York
2 June 2007

Dear Hank,

Nice long yellow letter [torn from legal pad] from you yesterday. I hope, first of all, that Adam finds a job he likes, Liz improves enough to discard the brace, and Casey-Jesse calms down after his procedure and spares the window from now on.

I'm glad you are cutting down a bit on the teaching by retiring from IUPUI at the end of the year. You could add to writing time and, dare I suggest it, rest or recreation. The big promotion of 1973 did it for me. I'm very happy you are promoted.

Congratulations to you. May, in a short time, your own fluffy white tail send appropriate signals back to the pack as you clear hedge after fence!

I remember when Dr. Rockwell gave me that promotion in his last budget in 1952, the Ph.D. year. The news got into Buffalo papers early, the day of my final orals at U.B. [University of Buffalo], and lengthened the faces of my examining committee, But, fortunately for me, the committee of an otherwise entrenched trio of Yale Ph.D. English professors also included Professor of Latin [Classics] Edward Grotrian Schauroth, [1888-1954; Author of *Observations on Vergil and His View of Life*, 1932, and holder of a 1910 A.B. degree from Harvard University], graduate of German universities. When he saw that the English professors had me on the ropes and were ready to kill, he cleared his Teutonic throat and took over since Latin was my minor and he had loved my written final exam in the poet Horace. He questioned me back to confidence while the Yale men glowered and I sailed through to the degree. Years later I was able to submit a little encomium to the UB column "Remember the Professor." Professor Schauroth's daughter and his friend, history professor [John T.] Horton [1920-1979], both sent me letters of appreciation. I treasure them, along with the letters from E.G.S., one of them in Latin.

Mentally, I seem ok. Physically, I force myself outside to walk with the blackthorn stick from Tralee. The garden is *gorgeous*, especially with huge Iris blossoms in every shade of blue and purple, plus red, brown and a beautiful shade of peach-pink. I have no energy and prefer a sleepy Fawn on my lap to any activity or company.

My father would be pleased that I have caught up with him. He died 16 September 1974, 22 days before his 94th birthday. I shall be 94, if I survive, in 21 days, on 23 June 2007. How I miss him, and my mother, who has been gone since 13 February 1953!

How lucky I was in my parents and my happy childhood in the hills of Vermont, and then in the succession of the University of Vermont, Duke University, and the Green Mountain College.

Enough already.

Love to you all.

Bob

PS: I sent a copy of the Tiger Rag article to Muriel Howard, who replied immediately in her customary delightful way. She concluded: "And thank you for leaving me with the thought of you dancing the Tiger Rag."

162. Nuwer to Drew
Waldron, Indiana
6 June 2007

Dear Professor Bob,

I like this [Edward] Hopper card at Le Bistro, 1909. Certainly the two stylishly clad madams would be fit faculty wives at Green Mountain—would they not? The woman wears pretty daring and dashing red garb for a faculty wife—but not for our Liz!

I have finished writing another book on writing. You should have in your hands by Halloween 2008, though I assure you there is nothing scary in there other than advice on avoiding dangling modifiers, my pet peeve as a teacher.

I now steal time from Vonnegut writing to edit Drew-Nuwer correspondence. I wanted the Drew-Nuwer edited correspondence to be your 94th birthday present (in addition to the Cuba book—*This Is Cuba: An Outlaw Culture Survives* by Ben Corbett). However, we two senior gents have created a mountain of written memories that stacked high might require me to borrow your blackthorn walking stick to clamber up the side of it. How's that for hyperbole?

I have been staying up past one a.m. and getting up at four or five a.m. to work on Drew/Nuwer and Kurt Vonnegut. I had fun addressing a Methodist church group in Lockerbie Square (Indianapolis) on the topic of Herr Vonnegut.

All is well here. Liz is having a little trouble sleeping with the marital bed empty half the night and husband and Double-Named Canine [Casey-Jesse] roaming at will on creaking floor. She just, at my request, made me an omelet and potatoes, delivered with a side lecture on cholesterol, while she pointedly ate only heart-safe Cheerios sweetened with banana.

Guilt!

Well, I'd better stop. Hi to Jim.

Love,

Hank

163. Drew to Nuwer
Waldron, Indiana
June 7, 2007

Professor Bob,

This is a second letter today.

If there is a writer's version of vertigo, I have it as I gallop ahead with our book at 9,000 words done. The vertigo comes from reading your own words and my own as I leap roles and decades from father, bullrider, bounty-hunter researcher, adventurer, scholar, teacher, son, husband, and so on. Did you ever see *Field of Dreams* where the author character played by James Earl Jones says "the one constant has been baseball"?

Well, for my part at least, the one constant in my life has been one Fraser Drew—believing, encouraging, grounding, and, gently admonishing (seldom if ever scolding or rebuking), and when needed, advising or consoling.

Maybe I am imagining it. But I think the Drew "persona" through 1979 was in some danger of either succumbing to ennui or flatness of personality caused by daily routine and imminent retirement. Somehow, I think, anyway (and you're entitled to screaming "poppycock" if you wish), your "wild" but focused students David Crosby, Tim Denesha, Tom Trainor, David Throne and Kevin Starr, Tom Hoar and Hank Nuwer with their antics, efforts and sheer gusto for life, literature, and making a difference, infused *you* their mentor with made-anew exuberance around age 66 or 67.

And guess what? *Your* energy came back at us through letters and visitations.

You will find an herb attached to this letter. I wish it were a secret Native American herb that you would sniff that might have you spring from the bed with bow and bowie knife in hand to find you a fresh buck for the hearth's stew kettle. But instead, maybe you will sniff it and get some pleasure of a far-off boyhood memory. It is the herb used to give licorice its scent and taste. I hope it isn't faded in scent by the time it reaches you.

The herb comes from the Greenfield garden of James Whitcomb Riley. His work is more from my pre-Drew elementary school days, of course. What a sad life his father had. Talented—a barrister, furniture maker, reader of great literature, pioneer, and great husband and father—he goes off to war and comes back shellshocked and debilitated. The family loses its house, and young Riley vows one day to buy it back. This he does, and he places another brother in that abode. Liz and I took a delightful break to go there for a two-hour tour of great gardens, magnificent old hickory trees, and the house itself. It had a wonderful two-sided partner's desk that Riley's father had made before the war for his partner and him. It was astonishing in workmanship and all the more charming for its flaws.

My writing day and night continues. If it isn't our project, it's the Buffalo novel or Vonnegut or Cornell hazing. I am sustained and happy when working on more than one project.

I'll write anon. You are not to worry one iota about replying. Give Jim my highest regard for all he does and let him know that he and you are in the thoughts of Liz and your old student. I'll close, as always, with Love and a signature.

Hank

165. Nuwer to Drew in Williamsville
Waldron, Indiana
13 July 2007

Dear Professor Bob:

I have been a little too acquainted with the night recently, going to bed when the werewolves start prowling on their appointed rounds and arising around 4 a.m.—around the time I imagine Robert Frost and Thomas Wolfe enjoyed nocturnal excursions respectively through field and city.

Violence, I hate to report, has come to Waldron.

Yesterday, it was fair Lizabeth who uncharacteristically leaped from bed to a) attend to my caffeine addiction and b) take the Dog with Two Names out to defile the morning glories.

Well, Liz has her list of fears, but maybe I haven't yet told you that the cloud of bats doubtlessly arising from some nearby limestone underground cavern every evening through morning has to be at the top of her phobia list. Telling her that Mr. and Mrs. Chiroptera pose no threat to her seems to offer her no reassurance.

So, the one day she jumps up to tend the dog while I perform a leisurely toilet (inside traditional bathroom sans morning glories), what happens?

You may have already guessed?

The one bat in Indiana who is not only blind but aerodynamically challenged flew onto our deck through the broken window opening created when aforementioned Dog with Two Names crashed through it.

Understand that to cool the dog I leave the old-fashioned whirling overhead fan going. Now, I have heard of demented cats leaping into such fans and being tossed through the air like a rolled morning newspaper, but I never had heard of a bat flying into one.

Never that is until Lizabeth stepped onto the deck and a flopping bat with undoubtedly a whopping headache landed at the feet of Casey-Jesse who darted and swooped and did his own impromptu imitation of a capeless matador. Frozen, and just a few inches from the dazed brown bat, Liz ordered yon Labrador to disobey his instincts and NOT retrieve at this time.

Unbelievably, he froze in place.

In another instant, the canine surely would have pounced and possibly made us very glad he had had a rabies shot. At that moment the bat regained its equilibrium, found its knocked-off fedora to tip goodbye to Liz, and flew back to the Bat Cave to tell how he alone had lived to tell the tale.

So, is this an end to the violence in Waldron, Indiana. Nay, dear sir.

Yesterday in the morning when I was taking the short walk to get the mail—which included a short note with an address label marked "Fraser Drew"—I stopped to admire the two baby mourning doves that had been hatched in a nest placed in the exterior rafters of our garage. They were perched atop my Subaru, using the top rack as a sort of viewing area, when a large mourning dove swooped out of the nearby blue spruce and missed one of the doves by a hair. Excuse me, by a feather. Must have been a love triangle gone wrong?

Not two hours later, I emerged from the house to find one of the young doves in the dirt trailing a broken wing like Robinson Jeffers's hurt hawk. I had no lead gift to provide, and it was making very fast time as it raced in a panic over a neighbor's grassy lawn toward the protection of some bushes. Whether it will recover like the bat, I do not know. But I will never consider the dove to be a symbol of peace ever again.

Thank you for your good note of July 10. It sounds as if you had lots of visitors. I'm glad you are hearing from old friends in nursing homes or in "custody" of much younger family members.

Thank you for striking all the typos I had inserted into our correspondence manuscript as a way of testing your copy editor skills. You passed with flying colors.

Thank you for your vigilance.

Some great news for January. The NCAA has put hazing as high on its list of priorities for the January convention. My friend Mary Wilfert there has done a good job. I have been such a vocal critic of Miles Brand (I really think he is a disappointment as both IU president and NCAA head) that I am not sure Mary politically can have me speak at the convention. She is, however, coming to my two classes to speak. [Ed. Nuwer was tapped to speak at the convention.]

In a few weeks I speak on high school hazing for my friend Elliot Hopkins, a near 300-pound former Wake Forest football captain who just got married for a second time and who is an executive with the National Federation of High Schools (a rules-making group for high schools covering athletics mainly, but also theatre, cheerleading, et al). I will have with me the parents of a young man who died in a hazing at the University of Miami. His name was Chad Meredith, and the parents were awarded $14 million. We are trying to get the Indiana law changed. It is now a pathetic, flimsy thing that cannot compare to California or New York law.

Yesterday, I took two hours completely for myself and played with some fiction—my old Buffalo novel manuscript. The hero is one Rev. Ezekial (Zeke) Ripulski, an amateur detective, a flawed but moral man, and pastor of a Buffalo church he desperately seeks to keep from the wrecking ball. Then there's a murder, and his whole day goes off kilter, especially seeing as how he's a suspect.

You were very much on the minds of Hank and Liz all this week. Liz and I rented a tearjerker (I love tearjerkers, sentimental slob that I am) called *Tuesdays with Morrie*. The book was written by Mitch Albom, and it was one of Liz's favorites. Albom was kind enough to answer some questions for one of my journalism students last semester, and that kind of interest in his own profession puts him on the "A" list in my book. Anyway, it was about a relationship between a student and his old professor—though that old professor (played by Jack Lemmon) was only 78.

It is time for yon drooling carnivore's breakfast, as well as my own— fresh-squeezed orange juice, poached eggs, and dry toast on the menu—even as my taste buds long for the forbidden taste of *huevos* and *chorizo* in fried corn tortillas heaped with flaming salsa.

Write from the gazebo if you have time. Hope the days there in Williamsville are far less violent than our own are here in Waldron. Liz's light step is outside the door, telling me it is likely daylight has peeked through our bedroom window. In another second she will ask what I am doing and send you her love, as do I now, friend Drew.

Hank

PS As I thumb through the letters you sent I spotted an envelope bearing a 25-cent stamp of Hemingway in green turtleneck with the veldt and a racing African antelope behind him. Has anyone in the U.S. Postal Department considered that the turtleneck might be wholly too warm for Africa safaris?

165. Drew to Nuwer
Williamsville, New York
23 December 2007

Your holiday present of the Buffalo Normal School Volume 1, Number 1, of the *Record* is a gem, and guess whom I found in the 1915 one—my colleague of early Buffalo State, Andy Grabau. He coached tennis and taught freshman English, especially to the sections of 1A boys in those days of sectioning. His wife was the charming Mary, nee Ludlow. After Andy's retirement the Grabows had Jim and me for Thanksgiving dinner once.

Best of all, 1915 included a student poem by Mary J. Doe. She taught third grade years later at School 52 in Buffalo, where Jim was very fond of her as his critic teacher. She and sister Bea were his friends and mine for the rest of their lives, and Jim visited Mary every day, even from Lockport, when she lived alone, found her a reliable cook-companion and arranged for her room in a good nursing home. She died at 96, leaving him her home, built by her father John Doe in 1920, and Jim and I lived there, 116 Crestwood Avenue, for several years. He is delighted to have this souvenir of his dear friend.

Love,

Bob

166. Drew to Nuwer

December 30, 2007

Dear Hank,

It looks as if I would hang on into 2008. I can see the stone in Randolph's older cemetery, a large and plain granite marker with DREW. In front are four smaller plain stones engraved:

Hazel Fraser Drew, 1889-1953

George Albie Drew, 1880-1974

Fraser Drew, 1913-

James A. Brophy, 1930-

It seems to me that 2008 will look much better after 1913 than 2007 would. Of course 2009 and 2010 are still possible but unlikely.

Also listed on this lot are Jim's parents, Beatrice Beckman, and my first cousin, Alice Gracelyn Drew. Gracelyn's father's lot was chockful of our grandparents and Uncle Leon's own family, and so I took her in so to speak. Bea was a very good friend who had nowhere to go and wished to be with Jim and me. All are properly designated.

End of necrological section.

Tomorrow we are invited for New Year's Eve dinner at Canterbury Woods by our dear friend on the staff who also arranged for our Christmas Day dinner, a magnificent repast.

I liked your having a Basque celebration at Christmas for Liz. My favorite entrée at the Chelsea Square Club House, which is open for Canterbury Woods residents Thursday-Sunday, is lamb chops or rack of lamb, and I like a local Greek restaurant which offers lamb shanks.

I envy you the [upcoming] Belgian trip. Have a great trip. Happy New Year to you and Liz and Casey and all outlying Nuwers.

Love, Bob

*Ed. This is the only letter Drew wrote with the month before the day in all his years of correspondence to Nuwer.

2008 Nuwer traveled to Brussels, the Ardennes and Luxembourg in January to complete research in Europe for his book on Vonnegut. He and co-author Jenine Howard resumed work on a project called *Young Musicians*.

Nuwer traveled to Spain and Nevada in May to research his novel-in-progress. He completed his coming-of-age novel *Back Country* set in Nevada and Guernica, Spain.

Alta Vista published Nuwer's *The Freelance Writer's Desktop Companion: Your Quick-Reference Guide to a Career As an Author.*

An earthquake shook Nuwer's hometown of Waldron. The town was struck by a June tornado, then flood days later. Nuwer and wife Liz volunteered with Red Cross to help victims.

Nuwer received honor from his peers as Franklin College scholar of year. The HazingPrevention.org "Anti-Hazing Hero Award" to honor individuals who show the courage to stop hazing was renamed the "Hank Nuwer Anti-Hazing Hero Award."

Nuwer appeared prominently in the Gordie Foundation's powerful documentary *Haze: The Movie.*

Nuwer and Drew completed *One Long Wild Conversation: Selected Letters Between a Buffalo State Professor and His Student, a Writer, 1970-2008*

167. Drew to Nuwer
Williamsville, New York
January 1, 2008

Dear Hank,

Happy New Year in my first letter of 2008. I wish you a great visit to the land of the Belgians and the rest of Europe. I hope that the Flemish-French-German speakers can cooperate well enough to preserve the little country. I can't imagine them splitting into three parts (like all Gaul in Caesar).

Good letter from you. I'll address your questions. I wrote Thornton Wilder first, out of my obsession with "The Bridge of San Luis Rey," which I read in 1927, when it first appeared with friend Arthur Jamieson on our stomachs on the floor of the Randolph apartment, he twelve and I fourteen. Twenty years later I wrote to Thornton Wilder and he responded 18 May 1947: "Mighty nice letter. A shot in the arm as I take up my daily stint on the new number which approaches its close."

And on and on about *The Ides of March*, his fourth novel. His friendliness led me to write others, including Hemingway in 1950 and Masefield in 1948.

Out of Masefield's courteous response developed my first big collection of books and letters, a dissertation, many articles and a book. Out of Hemingway's long and friendly response came several more letters, the best collection I have, and a serious influence on my teaching career.

I am a basically shy and diffident person, but the letters were easy to write. Going to meet the writers was difficult, and I had to push myself to meet Frost in Vermont, Hemingway in Cuba and less known Vermont and Irish writers.

Masefield was ill when I was in Masefield country in 1964 and we had only a brief telephone talk, which was not very satisfactory. I never talked with Jeffers or his family but had an excellent correspondence with sons Garth and Donnan, and several letters from Robinson Jeffers himself, Una, and a couple of grandchildren, as well as a long run of letters with Una's half-sister, Violet Hinkley.

I'll get this into mail with love and best New Year wishes. I recall New Year's Eve 1934-1935. I was visiting old UVM friend Betty Gray who had made reservations for us at the Hotel New Yorker, then posh and popular. The entertainers were the then wildly popular Ozzie Nelson and Harriet Hilliard, who came and sat with us for the intermission. It is all a lovely blur to me. Next morning I hitchhiked off south to finish my first year at Duke. I was twenty-one. Oh, my! As Grandma used to say.

Jim, Muts and I were dinner guests at Canterbury Woods main building dining hall last night—surf and turf. Nice visit with Harriet Vogelsang, Dr. Rockwell's younger daughter, now 81, afterwards. Muts and Jim partook of midnight herring here but I had crawled off to bed exhausted at 11 p.m.

Love to youse all!

Bob

168. Drew to Nuwer
Williamsville, New York
5 April 2008

Dear Hank,

This paper is so old that it crackles and tears easily, a hangover from St. Patrick's Day in the Sixties or Seventies. I assume that you are back safe and relatively sound from the Pyrenees. It is fortunate that you were not in Pamplona for the running of the bulls, for surely you would have been in the running and we all know how prone you are to some kinds of disaster. I seem to recall that the festival in question is in early July, the 6th maybe. I'm too lazy to turn the pages of *The Sun Also Rises* or to look up [the Festival of] San Fermin in my hagiographical dictionary.

I wish that your schedule and budget could have given you a look at Avila and Salamanca and Santiago de Campostela but we cannot always have everything that we wish.

Spain is certainly a complicated country, what with the Basques and Catalans and the people in the N.W. corner who are kin to the Bretons, Cornish, Welsh, Manx, Irish and Scots, I have always heard.

Everyone who knows Spain apparently loves it. I didn't have enough sense when I was in Ireland to fly over to Paris, so of course I didn't go to Spain. But I learned a hell of a lot about Ireland and had a good look at England & Scotland, then the Orkneys.

Greetings to all at home and afield.

Love,

Bob

169. Drew to Nuwer
Williamsville, New York
16 April, 2008

Dear Hank,

The week has begun pleasantly with two sets of visitors I enjoyed seeing, but even the happy occasions wear me out. Dave Crosby and Tim Denesha were here Monday for our usual lunch nearby and literary talk in my study—mostly Robert Frost and Wallace Stevens this time. We are all Frost enthusiasts, and I have been learning to admire the work of Stevens.

Incidentally, one of the top Wallace Stevens scholars is a former student of mine, John N. Serio of Clarkson University, whom I recall as a bright boy, but who did not get his Stevens addiction from my Contemporary Lit class. He is editor of the attractive *Wallace Stevens Journal.* Impressive even to a non-reader of Stevens.

Today, three ladies from my first Contemporary Lit class in fall 1945, with whom I have stayed in touch for sixty-three years, were here for lunch and had a lively visit. All are widows with four children each and many grandchildren. They are life-long friends and traveling companions on several continents and are now eighty-two. Jim likes them all and taught with one of them. Sue Marvin Flynn, one of yesterday's "girls," brought a large box of home-made cookies. Two,

Debbie O'Hagan Daly and Rita Lawler O'Brian, came with boxes of Watson's famous local chocolates, and so I shall be testing my character for many days—and losing the struggle.

Good luck with the Basque novel. Thanks for letter and beautiful Maine coast card. I thought at once of Edna Millay's youthful Maine poem "Renascence," which begins,

> All I could see from where I stood
>
> Was three long mountains and a wood;
>
> I turned and looked another way,
>
> And saw three islands and a bay.

170. Drew to Nuwer
Williamsville, New York
11 June, 2008

Dear Hank and Liz,

I don't like these TV pictures of rivers flooding towns in Indiana, but I am glad that there has been no special on Casey and his parents on a Waldron rooftop as the branches of fallen trees drift by. Seriously, I hope you escaped harm and property damage and that electric power has been restored.

The New York *Times* of 6 June has the obituary of Matthew J. Bruccoli of the University of South Carolina, 76 years old, the number one F. Scott Fitzgerald collector and Hawthorne expert. I have a couple of Bruccoli's publications and cherished notes.

Old students Tim Denesha and Dave Crosby came Monday on their monthly visit. We had a good lunch at the new Irishman's Pub in Williamsville and then a good session here on three poems of Matthew Arnold, W. H. Auden and contemporary Irish poet Michael Longley.

Love,

Bob

171. Nuwer to Drew
Waldron, Indiana
July 28, 2008

Dear Professor Bob:

Really enjoyed the recent letters. So glad that you made it to the Buffalo State reunion. Thanks to Vonnegut and classes and so on, I've been a bit of a prisoner of work these days.

Well my novel went through one more revision. It is now titled "Sheeps" and subtitled "A Coming-of-Age Novel of Guernica and Old Nevada." [*Ed. The title was changed to* Back Country.]

I sent it to the University of Nevada Press for my first preference, because they have such an extensive worldwide mailing list of Basques. They also occasionally publish fiction, though this is the exception, not the rule. Fingers crossed.

You now have the only copy of that novel draft. I destroyed the other copy so that I would not get it mixed up with the final cut and polish.

We are hanging in here. The railroad company has come back to service the once-abandoned tracks on our property because of the Honda plant being built nearby. They elected to trim trees on our property through the easement. They really butchered the top and our one-side heavy persimmon toppled in a windstorm. In addition, a neighbor had his roof caved in by a huge oak with amazing roots that came right out of the ground.

Liz is doing well. She is off at church getting a sewing lesson now. With costs up, she has become very creative with cooking on a budget. Actually, so have I. I made a bison chili, heavy on the rice and black beans, which was out of this world and allowed me to freeze two portions for future lunches.

My Vonnegut interviews with prisoners of war from Dresden have been as fascinating as they are enlightening and troublesome. They sure have my respect and thanks for all they endured. I hope to do another by phone today.

Casey has been good until yesterday. The neighbor bought a bunny rabbit and caged it. Casey is mesmerized and doesn't come when called. He sits transfixed in front of the cage like the two-year-old he is.

Summer classes are up next week and I have two weeks of Vonnegut here and in Newark, Delaware for Vonnegut and on to a Wilmington high school and then Clarkson University in New York State for hazing talks.

Well, Vonnegut chapter calls. So it goes. Or at least I go.

Adieu Professor Bob.

Liz sends love, as do I.

Hank

172. Drew to Nuwer
Williamsville, New York
13 August 2008

Dear Hank,

I am still processing in the weathered corridors of my brain all the intelligence with which you showered me in our phone conversation yesterday. Fawn and I are in the study. I am at my desk and she is snoring quietly on the couch, having finally accepted Jim's departure for the Shaw Festival's Niagara-on-the-Lake with Mutsuo.

Before I forget, I enclose a new reminiscence of old Ireland, this one about my probably deceased friend Sheila (Brigid) Murray. I have not heard from her in 10 years but she often comes to mind vividly when I look at her watercolors or wall-hanging, use her small brown cup from the Dunquin pottery, and pick up her novel.

This story of a 30-year friendship began with a cup of coffee in a little craft shop on the very edge of Europe in the summer of 1967. Jim Brophy and I were on our second trip to Ireland and had returned to the third of the three counties we had loved most in 1964— Donegal, Galway and Kerry. We had come back to Benner's Hotel, an old coaching inn in the capital of the Kingdom County, and were on a drive further west of Tralee to Dingle and Dunquin.

Out beyond the small seaport of Dingle the road goes *en corniche*, and from the dramatic turn at Slea Head the view is one familiar to moviegoers who saw *Ryan's Daughter*. The Blasket Islands lie off the coast, the "nearest [Catholic] parish to Boston"—Beginish, Inishtooskert, Inishnabro, Inishvickillane, the Tearacht and, largest of the six, the Great Blasket. I knew the story of the island community which had dwindled in 1953 to twenty adults and one child whom the government relocated on the mainland three stormy miles from the Great Blasket's tiny harbor. I had read English translations of the books of the islanders Tomas O'Criomhthain, Peig Sayers and Maurice O'Sullivan, and visitors John Synge and Robin Flower, and was eager to see where they had lived.

We stopped for information at the craft shop where two young women, Sheila Murray and Jean Yetts, served us coffee in their own pottery cups and told us of a man called Pound who occasionally, with two other fishermen, would row visitors out to the Blasket in a currach or niavogue, a canoe-like boat native to the Irish West. We found the men and had a memorable passage out to the Blasket and back in spite of threatening weather. The fare, from which our captain took his name, was one Irish pound for each of the rowers. This adventure, of which I have written elsewhere, gained us the approval of many Irish people, including the national hero and two-term President Éamon de Valera, with whom we later enjoyed an hour's conversation at the presidential mansion.

Back in New York, I wrote to thank Sheila and Jean for their recommendation of Pound. Sheila responded and a long correspondence, fueled by my later trips to the Irish Southwest, began.

Another of the joys of time in the far southwest was Sheila's cooking for meals at their later Craft Center or picnics on our delivery routes. I remember one dinner with the girls and two friends who were divers exploring the wreck of *Our Lady of the Rosary*, a Spanish Armada ship sunk in a Blasket Sound storm in 1588.

Karl and Kevin brought crayfish and lobsters from dangerous waters for the feast. One special picnic was high above Bantry Bay on a drive which took us over Tim Healy Pass from the Cork side of the Beara Peninsula back into Kerry. It was Sheila who drove me over Ballaghisheen Pass in Iveragh, while tourist coaches were following the coastal roads of the Ring. I went over my favorite Connor Pass on six of the seven Irish visits, three times in my friend's Land Rover.

My sheaf of Brigid's letters is thick. It contains many of her poems, all or nearly all unpublished. My last letter from her is dated 22 November 1998. She has not replied to several letters from me. Brigid had suffered from painful back injuries, treatments and surgeries, as well as other illnesses. From a visit to Lourdes, humbled by the sight of so many helpless people at the shrine which she called "the only place on the planet that gives the sick and disabled priority," she came away uncured but accepting her pain. "Maybe," she wrote, "that is the miracle."

I have much to anticipate here and on the many sectors of the broad Nuwer front. Stay well, both of you—all three of you, including poor wounded Casey.*

Love,

Bob

Ed. Casey survived an emergency operation after eating most of a throw rug one night.

173. Nuwer to Drew
Waldron, Indiana
August 15, 2008

Dear Professor Bob:

Appropriately, the last letter in this volume announces that we have climbed Suribachi, planted the Buffalo State flag on terra firma, and now deservedly may click heels or teeth in a glass, whatever seems most suitable.

The book, she is done. Compleat, as the old Angler might have written. I think that is all.

It has been a hard week for my mother in the hospital . She is confused and now thinks my Dad is still alive and cannot understand why he does not come. I am writing her obit this weekend—a sad task. I will do a humorous one, in addition, for the St. John Gualbert church service. Her monument with my dad is ready.

It was good to talk with you and Jim on the phone.

Casey is recovering from his self-spearing with the fallen tree limb when he dove into a pile of leaves like a kid on the last day of fall. He is an accident-prone dog. Must be a Nuwer.

How should I end this book? Perhaps by saying that your very last letter with its wonderful memories of the Blaskets and artist-writer Sheila Murray and the adventure-seeking Drew and Brophy provided the perfect ending for our book—linking other sections of the book discussing the Blaskets, Murray, President De Valera and the redoubtable Jim Brophy

And now I must print this testimony to more than 40 years of professor-student friendship that began when I went to your first class and you moved my desk to the front row right in front of you because I was flirting with a cute young lady.

I fly to Philadelphia on August 18 to interview the family of a prisoner of war who was shot by the Germans for stealing a teapot and is the partial model for the POW Edgar who suffered that dreadful fate in Slaughterhouse-Five. Then I take a rental car over to lecture to coaches and athletes on hazing in Wilmington, Delaware and top off the trip with eight hours of Vonnegut research at the University of Delaware.

Road trips. Research. Roaming. I guess that's the story of my life – and yours.

I begin teaching a week from Monday and have some of my favorite students enrolled. It should be a fun if busy semester.

At the end of the semester I look forward to research and literary snooping in Ireland, and I must be at least the hundredth student drawn to Eire by the Drew influence. I have my copies of Yeats and Joyce handy near the bed for brushing up. I land in Dublin via PSA at 11:10 a.m. on 23 January 2009.

That leaves only one thing to say. I have a title for our book, and it has a Robert Frost connection. I'd like to call it *One Long Wild Conversation: Selected Letters Between a Buffalo State Professor and His Student, a Writer, 1970-2008*.

As with all things between us, I hope you approve.

Love and friendship,

Hank

Appendix: Selected Listing of Key Persons

Aguilera-Hellweg, Max (1955-). Nationally known photographer who accompanied Nuwer on many magazine assignments, 1979-1981.

Brophy, James (1930-). Lifelong friend of Fraser Drew. Retired elementary school teacher, lover of the arts, world traveler, and Buffalo State College alumnus.

Cerniglia, Alice (1949-). An artist and arts administrator born 1949, she grew up in Brooklyn and attended Buffalo State 1967-1968 until marriage in 1968 to Hank Nuwer. Mother of Christian, Nuwer's firstborn son.

Collamore, H. Bacon ("Bac") Collamore, the friend to Frost and E.A. Robinson, who taught Drew much of what he knew about the craft of collecting books.

Drew, George Albie (1880-1974) was the father of Fraser Drew. He sold clothing at the Tewksbury and Raymond clothing store in Randolph, Vermont. He encouraged Fraser's pre-school reading and bought him two sets of encyclopedias at age eight.

Drew, Hazel Bell Fraser (1889-1953) was the mother of Drew. She could crawl well-smudged from under the Ford she was working on and emerge scrubbed and beauteous a few minutes later. She accompanied her son on excursions to the hills and brooks of central Vermont. Young Drew saw his mother's eyes fill with tears on November 11, 1918, after the armistice with Germany was signed to end World War One. His uncle, a Methodist deacon, and a local Catholic priest joyfully rang a church bell for hours to note the ceasefire.

Drew's dogs: He was a lover of dogs and during his lifetime enjoyed a long succession of them from a childhood Newfoundland to a Chihuahua at the end of his life.

—Bingo: white collie and Newfoundland mix, 1925-1938.

—Susie: black cocker and terrier mix, 1945-1958.

—Wolf: silver, tan and black German shepherd, 1965-1975.

— Lárach: black and tan Doberman pinscher, 1975-1983.

—Sugar: red miniature pinscher, 1981-1995.

—Sionnach: red miniature pinscher, 1983-1998.

—Shadey: red miniature pinscher, 1987-2002.

—Fawn: fawn-shaded Chihuahua, 1996-

Howard, Jenine (1951-). Born in North Carolina, she graduated from Indiana State University and became an editor. Mother of Adam Robert Drew, named after Professor Drew, who was born in 1985.

Klein Lizabeth (1958-). Born in New York City, she married Nuwer in Indiana in 2005.

Nicholl, Louise Townsend. Longtime friend to Drew and poet John Masefield, Drew visited her several times at her home in Scotch Plains, New Jersey, and she and her pianist sister Mary Florence Nicholl visited Drew's Randolph family home. Drew often brought her many drafts of a single poem to class as a way of demonstrating the creative process and the need for rewriting. Nuwer received a Nicholl poetry volume as a winner of a Drew Contemporary Literature Award, 1968. Nicholl was editor of the novels of Kentucky author Jesse Stuart, who in turn was a contributor to the University of Nevada literary magazine *Brushfire* when Nuwer was co-editor, 1973-1975.

Nikiel, Joseph. Nuwer lifelong friend and Buffalo State alumnus.

Nuwer, Henry R. (1915-1984). Father of Hank Nuwer. Worked as delivery driver in Buffalo. He was a farmer-turned-delivery man and, during World War Two, a tank driver with the Sixty-Sixth Armored

Regiment (Light), 2nd Armored Division. The elder Nuwer survived fierce World War Two fighting in North Africa, Belgium, Sicily, France and Germany, most memorably in the D-Day Landing and the Battle of the Bulge in the Ardennes. One of his commanders was Major Leonard H. Nason, author of books on military subjects such as *Three Lights from a Match* (1927).

Nuwer, Theresa (1919-). Mother of Hank Nuwer. Born in Black Rock section of Buffalo, New York in an apartment over the family store. After the store was sold she and her family moved to a farm on Westwood Road in Alden, New York. As a young woman she worked as a maid for Harry R. Templeton, president of the Ontario Biscuit Company, and his wife Gertrude Templeton; after that job she worked on an assembly line in an Ontario Biscuit plant. She married Henry R. Nuwer in 1945. She was a housewife through early 1970s, then a maid at the Sheraton Inn in Cheektowaga, New York, until her retirement in 1982.

Rockwell, Harry W., longtime president of Buffalo State, met job candidate Drew in 1945 under the clock at the Biltmore Hotel in New York after the president attended a concert on the final Friday of July. Rockwell interviewed the candidate from midnight until 2:30 a.m. In the morning Drew slept in the Hotel Commodore. A plane crashed into the nearby Empire State Building, jolting him while still in bed.

Tewksbury, Mary Carr. As a youngster Drew discovered the Kimball Public Library. Librarian Carr instilled in the Vermont boy a love of the ballads of the Middle Ages and Arthurian myth.

Tokaz, Edward (Tik). Boyhood and lifelong friend of Drew. Tik, just out of the University of Massachusetts, and Drew, just out of Duke, planned to go to Poland, where Tik still had an uncle in Czestochowa, and one in the port of Gdynia. The trip fell through when Tik got an appointment to Air Corps at Randolph Field, Texas, and Drew accepted an instructorship in Latin at Green Mountain College in Poultney, Vermont.

Photo Gallery

Thanks to several professional photographers who sold permission or generously granted Hank Nuwer permission to use their shots of him, including Jenine Howard, Dennis Cripe, Bob Horn, and Max Aguilera-Hellweg.

DOG DAYS: Fraser at 11 months of age with cousin Leo's bulldog, Ben (1913).

BEST FRIENDS: Fraser Drew at 15, with Bing (1928).

NEIGHBORS: Bob with Ginny, a Vermont neighbor (1931).

COLLEGE MAN: Bob as a sophomore at the University of Vermont (1930).

DUKE ROYALTY: Bob as a graduate student at Duke University (1934).

MOM KNOWS BEST: Fraser and mother in Hartford, CT (1943).

NEW TEACHER: Fraser and students during his first year of teaching at Buffalo State (1945).

COLLEAGUES: Fraser and Ruth Ryder, an exceptional education colleague (1949).

MID-CAREER PROFESSOR: Fraser at Buffalo State (1954).

DREW MEN: Fraser's father, George A. Drew, in Montpelier, VT (1966).

ROAD TRIP: Freshman team baseball players Larry Phelps, Dave Smolinski, and Hank Nuwer hang out at a motel following a game.

PUNCHED OUT: Hank Nuwer's identification card at Buffalo State.

IRELAND BOUND: Fraser boards an Aer Lingus flight on the second of his seven visits to Ireland (1967).

IRISH HERO: Left to right: Jim Brophy, President of Ireland Éamon de Valera and Fraser Drew enjoy audience (1967).
Photo credit: Fraser Drew

STUDY BREAK: Hank Nuwer and Alice Cerniglia attend Sigma Tau Rho party in 1967. They married in 1968.

CALL OF THE WILD: Fraser with his third dog, Wolf, in the Town of Tonawanda (1970).

SPECIAL STUDENT: Hank Nuwer's backup career was to work in special education. Here he works at a camp for youngsters with disabilities, Nevada, 1974. Photo credit: Bob Horn

PROUD MOMENT: Ernest L. Boyer, SUNY Chancellor, honors Fraser Drew, first BSC professor to be promoted to a Distinguished Teaching Professorship (1973).

FAN'S NOTES: Hank Nuwer signs autograph for Montreal Expos fan (1981).
Photo credit: Max Aguilera-Hellweg

TAKING A CUT: Hammering Hank Nuwer looks for a pitch in his wheelhouse
on a magazine assignment with the Montreal Expos minor league team (1981).
Photo credit: Max Aguilera-Hellweg

MAJOR INFLUENCE: Historical romance writer Rosemary Rogers wrote in a genre unfamiliar to Nuwer. But during their two years of dating (1979-1980), Rogers taught him to be ruthless with setting standards for the quality of his writing and to rewrite a book as many times as is needed to get every word right. Here they share a joke outside the New York City apartment of Rogers. Photo credit: Max Aguilera-Hellweg

GOOD FRIENDS: Fraser Drew meets Jenine Howard, mother of Adam Robert Drew Nuwer (1983). Photo credit: Hank Nuwer

FELLOW TRAVELERS: Fraser with long-time friend Jim Brophy in Woodstock, VT (1960).

NOTICE THE RESEMBLANCE? Adam Robert Drew Nuwer checks out his namesake, Fraser Drew, on first meeting (1986). Photo credit: Hank Nuwer

GETTING A LEG UP: Hank Nuwer and son Adam clown for camera in front of the Indiana University water fountain. Photo credit: Jenine Howard

NET GAIN: Hank Nuwer and son Chris are lifetime fishermen. Adam Nuwer maintains he fails to see the amusement in "tricking fish into committing suicide." Photo credit: Jenine Howard

ANOTHER WALK: Fraser walking with his sixth dog, Sionnach (1987).

SHOWTIME: Theresa Nuwer, Fraser Drew, and Adam Nuwer get early seating
for Hank Nuwer BSC Distinguished Alum award (1999).
Photo credit: Jenine Howard

SWISS OUTING: Screenwriter, producer, and lifelong friend Gian-Carlo Bertelli and Nuwer relax after a screenplay writing session in Switzerland (2005).

BEST BUDS: Hank Nuwer and long-time best friend Thelma Moore explore London (2005).

COWBOY UP: Hank Nuwer, who once "green-broke" his own horse and has profiled famed rodeo clown Leon Coffee, rode a bull in a rodeo at age 58 to write about it for a magazine. The result: seven broken ribs, a partially collapsed lung, and head abrasions. Two days later he went to New York for an interview on hazing with *Today Show* host Matt Lauer. Professor Drew and Nuwer's sons were not amused. Photo credit: Dennis Cripe (large photo)

MODEL PERFECT: Liz Klein Nuwer married Hank Nuwer in 2005.

NATIONALLY KNOWN BUFFALONIAN: Toyomi Igus (nee Gibson), a lifelong friend of Nuwer, was reared in Buffalo by her African-American father and Japanese mother. She met fellow Buffalo writer Hank Nuwer in 1976, and he profiled her in his award-winning *To the Young Writer*. Igus has written five award-winning children's books. She was a featured presenter at Buffalo State in 2004.

BSC FAMILY: Hank Nuwer relaxes at the BSC President's Home before receiving honorary doctorate of Humane Letters, 2006. L-R, Mickey Howard, Liz Nuwer, Muriel Howard, Hank Nuwer. Photo credit: Courtesy BSC

LAP OF LUXURY: Fraser in Williamsville with Fawn (2007).

TEXAS HOLD 'EM: Hank and Liz Nuwer try dancing Texas style in 2007.
Photo credit: Thelma Moore

Index